ROMANTICISM

INTRODUCTIONS TO BRITISH LITERATURE AND CULTURE SERIES

Medieval Literature and Culture
Andrew Galloway

Renaissance Literature and Culture
Lisa Hopkins and Matthew Steggle

Seventeenth-Century Literature and Culture
Jim Daems

Eighteenth-Century Literature and Culture
Paul Goring

Victorian Literature and Culture
Maureen Moran

Modernism
Leigh Wilson

Postwar British Literature and Culture 1945–80
Susan Brook

Contemporary British Literature and Culture
Sean Matthews

ROMANTICISM

Sharon Ruston

continuum

Continuum

The Tower Building
11 York Road
London SE1 7NX

80 Maiden Lane
Suite 704
New York, NY 10038

www.continuumbooks.com

© Sharon Ruston 2007

British Library Cataloguing-in-Publication Data
A catalogue record for this book is available from the British Library.

ISBN-10: HB: 0-8264-8881-1
        PB: 0-8264-8882-X
ISBN-13: HB: 978-0-8264-8881-7
        PB: 978-0-8264-8882-4

Library of Congress Cataloging-in-Publication Data
A catalog record for this book is available from the Library of Congress.

Typeset by Servis Filmsetting Ltd, Manchester
Printed and bound in Great Britain by MPG Books Ltd, Bodmin, Cornwall

Contents

Acknowledgements

I would like to thank a number of friends, colleagues and students who read and commented on parts of this book, particularly Chris Jones, James Kidd, Katherine Markham, Alison Parr, Dianne Pellicci, Anna Sandeman, Anne Sinclair and Peter Widdowson. My mum and brother, Bernadette and Gavin Ruston, read the whole book, and I'd like to thank them particularly for their help and corrections. The years spent teaching 'The Shelleys' Circle' at the University of Wales, Bangor, introduced me to some wonderful students, and gave me lots of ideas that have found their way into this book. I hope that the people who took that course remember it as fondly as I do. Writing the book, I have found a number of other guides particularly helpful, especially, *The Oxford Companion to the Romantic Age: British Culture, 1776–1832*, edited by Iain McCalman, and *Romanticism: An Oxford Guide*, edited by Nicholas Roe. Of course, any mistakes found in this book are my own. The book is dedicated to Jerome de Groot, whom I love very much.

Note on the text:
Quotations are taken from the eighth edition of *The Norton Anthology of English Literature* (2006). If the text being referred to is not in this volume I have quoted from the third edition of *Romanticism: An Anthology*, edited by Duncan Wu (2006).

Introduction

What is Romanticism? It is a notoriously difficult term to define, made more complex by the amount of recent critical work which has discovered new dimensions to Romanticism, many of which seem to contradict each other. 'Romanticism' is not a term that was used by the writers whom we now designate as Romantic; it is a label that has been applied posthumously and with hindsight. It is doubtful whether writers at the time would have felt that they had much in common with each other in terms of their politics, religious beliefs and aesthetic theories. Yet, P. B. Shelley (1792–1822), William Hazlitt and John Stuart Mill all spoke with confidence of a 'spirit of the age', something they felt distinguished their times from others.

Romanticism is often defined in terms of its historical period but the exact dating of this period is a matter of some dispute. The sense the Romantics had of themselves as different from their predecessors was in large part due to the events that they witnessed, events which themselves did not seem to have a precedent. The ideals of the American and French Revolutions, enshrined in their declarations of independence and the rights of man, spoke of the equality of all men, something we now, perhaps, take for granted but which was not always the case. Indeed, even then, when the equality of 'man' was argued for, many writers argued for more than this, for equal rights for black people (slavery was not abolished until the end of this period in 1833) and for women. There is an argument, therefore, for defining Romanticism by its origins. In this book, I consider the effect of the American and French Revolutions but also earlier works and events that might be considered influential in bringing these Revolutions about, such as the writings of Jean-Jacques Rousseau and the philosophy of the Enlightenment.

Another way to limit or define Romanticism chronologically would be to look to the end of the period; the reform acts of the 1830s are often considered to reflect a shift in government. These reforms may well have saved Britain from its own revolution, which at different points during the Romantic period had seemed imminent. In the 1790s and 1810s, in particular, Britain had been ruled by oppressive forces, with 'Gagging Acts' passed to silence the radical press, the setting up of spy networks to inform on and even instigate revolutionary activity, which would then be punished harshly with transportation or execution, and acts passed to stop people meeting to discuss the economic hardships they were suffering under. Despite this, there were marches to demand that the Government take action, petitions to Parliament and riots. The events of 16 August 1819, which were given the name of 'Peterloo', demonstrate the way that Lord Liverpool's Government dealt with those who were asking for reform: a peaceful demonstration of unarmed men, women and children at St Peter's Fields, Manchester was broken up by horsemen with sabres who killed at least ten people and injured hundreds of others. The attackers were publicly thanked by the Home Secretary when he was informed about what had happened. The name Peterloo made reference to the country's recent triumph against Napoleon at the Battle of Waterloo, and clearly suggested that the Government was waging war on its own people. During the Romantic period Britain was at war almost continually, first with revolutionary France and then with Napoleonic France. These years are characterized by economic depression, poverty, food riots, machine breaking, paranoia and repression. Another way to think of Romanticism, then, is as a period of political polarization, with politically radical writers such as William Godwin

(1756–1836), Mary Wollstonecraft (1759–97) and others living in fear of imprisonment, their writings represented in the Tory press as unpatriotic, immoral, blasphemous and seditious.

The writing produced within this time can be seen as revolutionary. The term Romanticism, rather than explicitly referring to a historical period, such as eighteenth-century or Victorian literature, suggests a literary or artistic movement. Joanna Baillie (1762–1851), a dramatist, argued for naturalness in literary language in her 'Introductory Discourse' to *Plays of the Passions* (1798), and this call was taken up by Wordsworth (1770–1850) and S. T. Coleridge (1772–1834) in the 'Preface' to the 1800 edition of *Lyrical Ballads*. There is the distinct sense among these writers that they are doing something new; the air of excitement is palpable. Romanticism can be thought of as an attempt at sincerity and genuine feeling, writing about emotion in the 'real language of men', as Wordsworth put it (Norton 2006, vol. 2, 262). The conversation poems of Coleridge or Anna Barbauld (1743–1825), the confessional mode of Wollstonecraft's *A Short Residence in Sweden*, and the strong attachment of John Clare (1793–1864) to his home, all offer examples of both 'real language' and 'powerful feeling' (Norton 2006, vol. 2: 262, 265). This can be contrasted, though, with another prominent strain in Romantic writing – the witty, urbane voice of Byron (1788–1824), for example, who uses satire and irony to convey his cynicism towards the world. Not all writers of the period considered the line broken between their eighteenth-century predecessors and themselves; where Wordsworth railed against the neo-classical ideas of art, Byron greatly admired the poetry of Alexander Pope and John Dryden.

It has been also argued that Romanticism can be divided along gender lines. Masculine Romanticism is seen as typified by Wordsworth, represented as concerned with nature rather than society, introspective, and looking beyond the material world to something transcendent. Feminine Romanticism, on the other hand, it has been argued, celebrates the domestic affections, family and social bonds. Wordsworth is often prominent in definitions of Romanticism; for many he is the archetypal Romantic, although this ascendancy is largely the effect of a later period's canonization of his poetry. The myths of Romanticism still exist today, with the idea of the Romantic poet as a 'romantic' in the sense of someone who idealizes the past or present, who is not socially engaged with his contemporary world, who communes with nature to the detriment of any political responsibility. The historicist research that has been done in the previous decades (discussed in Chapter 3 of this book) has revealed that this is a myth, even in the case of John Keats (1795–1821), a poet who has been considered as merely 'escapist'.

The centrality of poetry in a definition of Romanticism has also been debunked. In fact, Romantic drama was vibrant during the time, and even those writers known primarily for their poetry wished that they could write a successful play to be performed at Drury Lane or Covent Garden. Again, historicist research has given us a more accurate picture of which writers were most successful at the time, not Shelley or Keats, but Baillie and Felicia Hemans (1793–1835). Women were prominent in all genres, but it is indicative of the sexist and hierarchical criteria upon which writers of the past have been judged that the popular genres of the novel and drama have been neglected and their importance only recently recovered. The novel became very popular during this period, and was a form written and read by women in particular; the consumption of novels was encouraged by an increase in literacy, circulating libraries and new printing technologies. Many more books were published than in previous ages. The Gothic novel was one form that emerged in this period and which continues to this day. Aiming to invoke a 'pleasing horror' in its audience, these books tapped into the fears and concerns of the reading public, with stories of ignorance, superstition, repression and tyranny. In the past, Romantic poetry was privileged above other genres as the product of six white male geniuses, who were appreciated precisely because they were believed to exist somehow outside their historical moment and were inspired by other-worldly forces. Today, Romantic literature is a term which is used far more inclusively, and which can be seen to reflect the political events of the period.

One role that literature played, as part of Romantic culture, was to encourage and challenge a sense of national identity and nationhood. Indeed, the concept of nation, as we now understand it, is one that emerged around this time. A nation has been described as an 'imagined community', often defined by imaginary rather than real geographical borders. During almost continual war with France, when Britain was seriously afraid of an invasion, whether from France itself or from French allies in Ireland, and when the Act of Union formed the 'United Kingdom' as we now know it, the idea of Britain as a nation was formed. The Union Jack flag was first used in 1801 to symbolize this new nation, and stereotyped characters representing the English and the French in political cartoons were instrumental in developing a national identity.

Tory publications, such as the *Anti-Jacobin*, campaigned against those it labelled **'Jacobins'*** who supported the ideals of the French Revolution, liberty, fraternity and equality, accusing writers of unpatriotic feelings towards Britain. There were also anti-Jacobin novels that continued this propaganda, promoting ideals of tradition, hierarchy and property. Competing ideas of nationhood emerged in the novels about Ireland of Sydney Owenson and Maria Edgeworth and the novels about Scotland of Walter Scott. The losses and gains of the British Empire during this period, with Britain acquiring colonies across Asia and Africa by the end of the Napoleonic wars, were also a part of this nation formation. Literature in this period can be found that either reflects or challenges the nation's dominant ideologies, either celebrating the Empire or criticizing the imperialist agenda. Anna Barbauld's poem *Eighteen Hundred and Eleven*, written in that year, prophesies that eventually Britain's power will fail

---

* Terms in bold indicate that they can be found in the glossary, p. 131.

and be lost. She imagines a time when England will be only 'grey ruin and mouldering stone' and draws a direct comparison with the colonies, England will then 'sit in dust, as Asia now' (Wu 2006: 46–7). This poem received such vitriolic criticism that Barbauld stopped writing poetry. For the first time, in these decades, the marginalized voices of former slaves are heard, as well as other disenfranchised groups, arguing for their rights. Religious dissenters and Catholics fought and finally won battles for toleration, and the animal rights movement began.

As long ago as 1924, A. O. Lovejoy wrote that we should use the plural term 'Romanticisms' rather than refer to a singular Romanticism:

> The word 'romantic' has come to mean so many things that, by itself, it means nothing. It has ceased to perform the function of a verbal sign. When a man is asked [. . .] to discuss romanticism, it is impossible to know what tendencies he is to talk about, when they are supposed to have flourished, or in whom they are supposed to be chiefly exemplified. (Lovejoy 1970: 66–7)

I hope in this book to give some idea of the many Romanticisms that are available to us, to show the points at which Romantic writers come together and where they diverge. If there is any coherence to be found among these writers, it is in their own belief that what they were doing was new, whether this is referring to their new sense of the need for equality and enfranchisement, a new understanding of the role of the poet, a belief in the limitlessness of science's potential achievements, a new interest in the forgotten and neglected people of society, a new fascination with the dark, unexplored regions of the psychological, mysterious and supernatural. Of course, as *we* change so does our perception of the Romantics, but right now issues of human rights, religious toleration, nationalism, social responsibility and the role of art in society seem very contemporary indeed.

1

Historical, Cultural and Intellectual Context

Politics and Economics
Philosophy and Religion
Science and Technology
Arts and Culture

POLITICS AND ECONOMICS

Beginning with reference to the American War of Independence, and moving on to a discussion of the French Revolution and war between Britain and France, this section considers the new language of 'rights' that this period created. The rights of men, women, slaves and even animals are discussed within this context of political upheaval and uncertainty, tracing the idea back to Jean-Jacques Rousseau's notion of primitive man. This section examines events in the colonies of Britain, in the West Indies and India particularly, rebellion in Ireland, the threat of invasion from France and the Act of Union (1801), leading up to the Abolition of Colonial Slavery in 1833. The work of Adam Smith, *Enquiry into the Wealth of Nations* (1776) was extremely influential in this period, beginning the trend in free-market economics which has continued to this day, while Thomas Malthus's predictions for the geometric rise in populations fed conservative hysteria. This section briefly considers the cost of living for those in the labouring classes during this time of Industrial Revolution, times of bad and good harvest, looking at the

Luddite and machine-breaking movements leading up to political reform and the repeal of the Corn Laws in 1845.

The American Revolution

Depending on the political views of those involved, the years of the Romantic period were considered either times of great optimism when liberty spread across America and Europe and human rights were being openly discussed and enshrined in the constitutions of fledgling democracies, or as dark days in which the threat of revolution was always present to challenge status, property, traditional hierarchies and security. The American Revolution and War of Independence (1775–83) was viewed in many different ways: applauded by some who encouraged America to throw off the yoke of its British oppressor but condemned by others who regarded it as a lessening of British power, trade and world reputation. In Thomas Paine's book *Common Sense* (1776), he called for America to free itself from Britain, arguing that a government based on inheritance (in which power is passed down from generation to generation, as it is in the case of the English monarch or the House of Lords) was tyrannous, and that the claim that it was fair was 'farcical' (Paine 1995: 8).

The result of the American rebellion was the loss of the American colonies – and this hit Britain hard. The deciding factor had been the taxes that the British Government demanded of the 13 states, and the question of how to control colonies elsewhere after the War of Independence had been lost was one with which Britain continued to have difficulties. America, though, was depicted as the land of the free, and for this reason was the place that Joseph Priestley fled to when he was attacked by the so-called Church and King mobs in 1791. For similar reasons, the poets Coleridge and Robert Southey planned a scheme to emigrate to the Susquehanna river in Pennsylvania, near Priestley, that they called 'pantisocracy'. They imagined a commune-style life based on principles of equality, with the community equally sharing wealth and property. In the early 1780s, the situation in America led people to look again at the British constitution and to ask for parliamentary reform, though this abated after Prime Minister William Pitt the Younger's moderate reforms seemed to mollify such calls and to restore confidence in the Government.

The French Revolution

There were tangible links between the events that unfolded in America and the events of the French Revolution, not least in the person of Thomas Paine, whose *Rights of Man* (1791–2) defended the revolution in France. Thomas Jefferson, the third President of the United States, also had firm political links with France, serving there as the American Minister. The overthrow of the *ancien régime* in France, a political system that encouraged decadence and luxury legitimated by the absolute rule of the king, was almost universally heralded in Britain. News of the fall of the Bastille, a prison in Paris, on 14 July 1789 was greeted with enthusiasm and approbation. Britain regarded itself as possessing a fairer constitution than France, with its three-tiered system of 'checks and balances' enforced by the monarch, the House of Commons and the House of Lords. The French Revolution was, in general, regarded in Britain as catching up with the progress that had been made since its own bloodless 'glorious revolution' of 1688, when the present system, called constitutional monarchy, had been established. Wordsworth visited France twice during the revolutionary period, and looking back on these times in *The Prelude* declared, 'Bliss was it in that dawn to be alive, / But to be young was very heaven!', while Percy Shelley, who was only born in 1792, described the French Revolution as the 'master theme of the epoch in which we live' (Norton 2006, vol. 2: 374; Shelley 1964, vol. 1: 504). Mary Wollstonecraft and Helen Maria Williams were among the British writers who lived for a period in France during these heady days.

Amidst this pro-revolutionary feeling in Britain, Edmund Burke's *Reflections on the Revolution in France* (1790) at first

seemed out of place. Burke wrote his *Reflections* in the form of
a letter 'Intended to Have Been Sent to a Young Gentleman
in Paris' who had asked him what he thought of the events
occurring (Norton 2006, vol. 2: 152). In his answer, Burke
referred to the Revolution as an unnatural action and as a
kind of disease, liable to spread across the water to England.
He emphasized the violent aspects of events, offering a sen-
sationalist account of the intrusion of a Parisian mob into the
bedchamber of Queen Marie-Antoinette, who was depicted
by Burke in sentimental style as 'glittering like the morning-
star, full of life, and splendour, and joy' (Norton 2006, vol. 2:
156). The remembrance of her present suffering provokes
Burke to exclaim: 'little did I dream that I should have lived
to see such disasters fallen upon her in a nation of gallant
men, in a nation of men of honour and of cavaliers' (Norton
2006, vol. 2: 156). As this overblown and melodramatic
account makes clear, Burke firmly believed in the chivalric
code, in hierarchy, and in inherited wealth and power, not in
natural rights for all regardless of their status or position.
While it may have seemed out of kilter with general sentiment when it was first published, as the French Revolution
became more violent and the guillotine claimed increasing
numbers of victims, *Reflections* was regarded as strangely
prophetic. The British were increasingly nervous of France
when it seemed to go further than the 1688 Revolution had
done, when King Louis XVI and Queen Marie-Antoinette
were taken to the guillotine and the Reign of Terror brought
news of terrible atrocities. France also began looking to
expand its borders, and finally, in February 1793, Britain
declared war on France.

The demand for rights

Burke's *Reflections* provoked a pamphlet war, with over a
hundred responses to it published, one of which was Paine's
Rights of Man (1791–2). Burke refused to believe that 'natural
rights', the inalienable rights that all possess, could be the
basis of a society. In fact, even those who asserted their

support for natural rights were often ignoring whole sections of a society. When Charles-Maurice de Talleyrand-Périgord presented his report on public education to the National Assembly in France, he advocated, for example, that girls should be educated in domestic duties only. Wollstonecraft pointed out in her *A Vindication of the Rights of Woman* (1792) that this did not live up to the promise of the revolutionary ideal that asserted rights for all. Indeed, it seemed to Wollstonecraft that the *Declaration of the Rights of Man and of the Citizen* precisely and specifically concerned men, not in a sense that included all human beings but in one that, in fact, actively excluded women. She felt that women should be entitled to what she called, the 'natural rights of mankind' (Wollstonecraft 1997: 104). In *Reflections*, Burke had written that once the 'decent drapery of life is to be rudely torn off' from our 'naked shivering nature', we realize that 'a king is but a man; a queen is but a woman; a woman is but an animal; and an animal not of the highest order' (Norton 2006, vol. 2: 157). Wollstonecraft attacked what she saw as Burke's problematic formulation of women as animals who were fundamentally different from men in her *Vindication of the Rights of Men* (1791), instead arguing that women and men should all be regarded as part of mankind (Wollstonecraft 1997: 56).

A similar situation existed in contemporary accounts of race, where the European was placed above the African on the physical and intellectual scale. Rights were also being asserted for slaves during this period, when, even after losing colonies in America, Britain still held colonies in Asia and Africa which were important for trade. Importing black slaves, mainly from Africa, to work on the British-owned sugar plantations in the Caribbean was a crucial factor in the trading power and immense wealth of the British Empire. In a literary representation of this, in *Mansfield Park* (1814) by Jane Austen (1775–1817), Sir Thomas Bertram visits the plantation he owns in Antigua, the source of his family's wealth. Slaves were treated inhumanely, living in the most awful conditions, even if they managed to survive the horrific journeys from their homelands, from which they had often been kidnapped. Upon Sir Bertram's return, Fanny asks him about the slave trade and her enquiry is met with silence. Much has been made of this event in the novel, particularly given Fanny's problematic position in the Bertram household where she is regarded by many in the family in the role of a servant rather than an equal. In these respects, *Mansfield Park* has been seen as a criticism of the British aristocracy, represented as morally dissolute and decadent.

The anti-slavery movement was formalized by the founding of the Society for Effecting the Abolition of the Slave Trade in 1787. The Society was mostly made up of those from the Quaker religion, but quickly managed to get thousands of names for petitions to abolish the slave trade abroad. They appealed particularly to the notion of a Britain that valued principles of liberty and humanitarianism. The cult of sensibility (explored at greater length in Chapter 2), with its emphasis on sympathizing with others, meant that slavery was one area of politics in which women were permitted to play a role. Hannah More and Ann Yearsley were among the diverse range of female poets who wrote against the slave trade. On the island of St Domingue in 1791, there was a slave rebellion in which slaves burned plantations, killed their French masters and achieved freedom and independence (the island declared itself as the free republic of Haiti in 1804). In 1807, the Abolition of the Slave Trade Act was passed, abolishing trade in slavery and fining those who continued to trade in slavery £1,000 per slave. When slavers were caught by the British navy, they often threw slaves overboard to avoid being heavily fined. It was not until 1833 that slavery was finally outlawed in British colonies.

The Revolutionary and Napoleonic Wars

The Revolutionary Wars began in 1793 after France declared war on its neighbouring countries, Austria and Prussia, which were threatening to invade, and continued till the Peace of Amiens was reached in March 1802. This period of peace lasted only 14 months, until May 1803, when the Napoleonic Wars began between Britain and France, now led by Napoleon Bonaparte, who seemed to have returned the country to a dictatorship much like the absolute monarchy the Revolution had originally fought to overthrow. These wars have been seen as different from those that had gone before in a number of important respects: the countries involved were mobilized to a degree not hitherto witnessed, as unprecedented numbers joined the armed forces and civilians played their role in protecting their home country from potential invasion. Also, these wars were fought primarily on ideological grounds rather than for territory, though Britain was still trying to secure new colonies while hanging on to the old ones, pursuing an increasingly imperialist agenda for its growing Empire.

For both France and Britain, the wars focused the country's attention on what it meant to be French or British, as concepts of nation were created and developed. Timothy Baycroft, in *Nationalism in Europe, 1789–1945*, has argued that the French Revolution was the birth of the modern nation (Baycroft 1998). It marked a time when the people of the French nation rose up against their oppressors (the Bourbon monarchy and the *ancién regime*) and formed a nation-state, replacing the old idea of a divinely ordained law regulated by the king with a republic. France was to be governed by its people, or at least their representatives. The new French nation then began to wage war on those who opposed liberty and sought to liberate other oppressed peoples in other nations. The French army was very different from its English counterpart, many of whom had been forcibly press-ganged into joining the forces. French soldiers, in contrast, were motivated by patriotic and rousing songs and political speeches. There were other wars for independence during the Romantic period, such as Corsica's bid for independence in 1793, the Greek War of independence begun in 1821, and a number of nation-states or republics emerged, including America, France, Venice, Genoa and Milan.

In response to France's developing sense of nationhood, Britain's idea of itself also became more coherent and unified. This was particularly helped by increased levels of literacy and new print technologies, which enabled political news to reach a large audience. When fears of a French invasion were at their height, particularly in 1796–8 and 1803, Britain as a nation was roused by a patriotic cry to defend its borders, both physical and ideological. The Act of Union (1800), which formally united Ireland to England by dissolving the Irish Parliament and moving political representatives for Ireland to the House of Commons in London, set up free trade between the two countries but also demanded that the Irish pay a colonial tax to England. The Society for United Irishmen had been founded in 1791 by Wolfe Tone, an association of Protestants and Catholics who wanted an Irish republic and were prepared for rebellion. In 1796, Tone persuaded the French to send an expedition to Ireland, and though the ships reached Bantry Bay, they were unable to land due to the poor weather conditions. In 1798, rebellion occurred in Ireland and the French landed in Mayo, attempting to assist the rebels. Despite some early successes, French expeditions failed and the rebels were eventually defeated. As a later section of this chapter will show, the Romantic period saw cultural revivals in England, Ireland, Wales and Scotland as these countries attempted to establish independence from each other and distinct national identities.

Economics

Questions of taxation were much discussed during this period, whether they involved the politics of taxing a colony overseas, the taxes endured by the labouring poor in Britain or the taxes imposed on goods imported into Britain. In 1775, Adam Smith had published a book that formed the basis for modern economics, *The Wealth of Nations*. He argued that any kind of government legislation that restricted or protected the price of goods was working against the expansion of trade. He advocated, therefore, a **laissez-faire** system of government which allowed markets to find their own price. Smith acknowledged that self-interest was largely the governing force behind the decision to make certain goods, that people would only make those goods they felt they would gain most profit by, but he believed that unrestrained competition within the marketplace would ensure that goods reached their 'natural price', thus also benefiting those who needed to buy them. Britain had traditionally operated on a mercantilist system that encouraged exports and discouraged imports through a system of tariffs. Smith was instrumental in persuading Britain to adopt a free-trade policy, which instead allowed for goods to pass between countries untaxed. In 1815, after a bad harvest, when the price of corn produced in England was high because it was so scarce, the Government introduced the Corn Laws, an import tariff that made corn that had been imported from overseas too expensive for British people to buy. The Corn Laws benefited the aristocracy, whose money came from the land, and greatly increased the suffering of the lower classes, who could not afford to buy bread. Indeed, during the Romantic period, episodes of economic depression and the cost of the war effort resulted in serious political unrest, which seemed to many to suggest that there would be a revolution in Britain just as there had been in France. In fact there was no revolution, though there were major disturbances. The Repeal of the Corn Laws in 1846 was one of the measures brought in to help the Irish peasants at the beginning of the potato famine.

Even at the start of the Romantic period, Britain had a huge national debt, and this grew even larger during the war years, until in 1815 debt repayments accounted for around a third of the Government's expenditure. Successive governments attempted to reduce the debt by using a number of means. Indirect taxes on goods such as tea, candles, salt, tobacco, sugar, alcohol and soap were imposed, where the price of the goods was inflated to cover the cost of paying taxes to the Government, again hurting the consumer of these goods most. Bricks, timber and glass were taxed so that their cost increased, too. Four Stamp Acts were introduced between 1793 and 1815, imposing taxes on a number of printed items, including, in 1815, newspapers, thus effectively silencing the radical press. In an attempt to raise money for the impending Napoleonic Wars, Pitt introduced the extremely unpopular income tax (1798–9) on incomes over £60 a year; it did not raise the £10 million he hoped for and was abolished during the Peace of Amiens, only to be re-introduced when the war began again, and abolished again after Napoleon's defeat at Waterloo in 1816.

Another source of concern during this period was the dramatic rise in population, which, in England, more than doubled between 1771 and 1831. There was a serious worry that the land would be unable to provide enough food for the number of mouths that needed to be fed now. This, at least, was the argument of Thomas Malthus, whose *Essay on the Principle of Population* (1798) was one of the texts that inspired Charles Darwin's *The Origin of the Species* (1859). Malthus argued that population increased at a rate that could not be matched by increases in the production of food, and that natural or unnatural controls were needed to check growth in population. The kinds of events he was referring to were wars, natural disasters, disease epidemics and a whole host of problems associated specifically with the living conditions of the poor, such as unhealthy environments, dangerous working conditions, insufficient food, large families and poor medical treatment, all of which combined to shorten life expectancy. Malthus's strictures on the need for moral restraint among the poor, encouraging them to practise celibacy even during marriage, drew fierce opposition.

Riots and reform

The food riots in England from 1794 to 1796 were a direct result of the worsening living conditions of the poor. Indeed, historians now believe that the years following the bad harvests of 1794–5, 1799–1800 and 1810–11 were periods of famine in Britain (Wells 2001: 504). At such times the difficulty of procuring the means to live provoked political agitation; riots often concerned requests for increased wages, the need to lower the cost of food and the lack of employment, and were accompanied by shouts of 'Bread or Blood'. Most of a farm labourer's income went on buying food for himself and his family, and when he was out of work he had to rely on poor relief (raised by the 'poor rates' tax on the affluent). Disturbances were also caused by the increased number of turnpike trusts – these were tolls imposed for the upkeep of a road on the people who used them. This, coupled with the increased enclosure of what had previously been common ground that could be used by anyone to graze cattle or gather firewood, meant that the rural poor had a much harder time making ends meet. The poetry of John Clare reveals the damaging effects of enclosure on the labouring classes.

There were other types of employment in the emerging cities; factory work was dictated to by other pressures, such as the demands, or lack of demand, of trade, and was accompanied by awful living conditions, including long working hours and squalid housing. The so-called Luddite movement, named after their mythical leader Captain Ned Ludd, attacked and destroyed machines that were intended to replace human labour, particularly in the trades of weaving or stocking-making. In 1811 and 1812 the Luddites targeted wool and cotton mills in the north-east of England. The army were employed to stop them after machine-breaking had been made a capital offence – punishable, in other words, by death. In his maiden speech in the House of Lords, Byron argued against this bill. Luddites caught were dealt with harshly; men were executed and many others transported to Australia after trials in 1812 and 1813. All popular uprisings were dealt with harshly, such as the Pentridge march on Nottingham in June 1817, led by Jeremiah Brandreth, which resulted in the execution of three and the transportation of many others. Trade Unions were prohibited by the Combination Acts of 1799 and 1800, although such activities were often pursued under the guise of friendly societies or clubs.

These uprisings were not simply due to economic factors: the Pentridge uprising had a number of demands to make of Parliament. Brandreth had been persuaded to gather together the 300 men who marched to Nottingham by a man who was secretly in the employ of the Government, one of the Home Secretary, Lord Sidmouth's spies, an *agent provocateur*. These spies infiltrated radical circles, encouraged disgruntled men to plan insurrection and then informed on them to the Government. This 'Committee of Secrecy' was part of the repressive measures that Lord Liverpool's Government employed to forcibly crush rebellion. Wellington's defeat of Napoleon at Waterloo in June 1815 had not brought the prosperity that people had expected, and when servicemen returned home unemployment figures rose. Liverpool had tried and failed to retain income tax and money had to be found from high indirect taxes. Rather than appease calls for reform, the Government decided to repress them just as they had in the 1790s when a similar situation had existed.

As long ago as 1780, people had been calling for reform; the Society for Constitutional Information demanded universal male suffrage, something that was not achieved in Britain till 1918. Before the Reform Bill of 1832, 15 per cent of British men had the vote, the qualification for which still depended upon the land they owned, and this effectively disenfranchised most British people. There were also campaigns for the right to a secret ballot, thus removing the possibility of bribery and bullying, such as that described in the case of Hawkins, in William Godwin's novel *Caleb Williams*. Hawkins, the holder of a 'small freehold estate' which enabled him to vote in local elections, also rented a farm from a Mr Underwood, a local squire and therefore gentry: 'a warmly contested election having occurred, he was required by his landlord to vote for the candidate in whose favour he had himself engaged. Hawkins refused to obey the mandate, and soon after received notice to quit the farm he at that time rented' (Godwin 1982: 66). When Hawkins appealed to another squire, Mr Tyrrel, to take him in, Tyrrel is at first unpersuaded, telling Hawkins: 'you know it is usual in these cases for tenants to vote just as their landlords please. I do not encourage rebellion' (Godwin 1982: 67).

Another cause for concern was the existence of so-called 'rotten boroughs', places that were represented by a Member of Parliament (MP) but which had only a few voters. One such village was Gatton, which until 1832 returned two MPs even though the village had only 23 houses and 11 voters. These were contrasted with the new large urban areas such as that of Manchester and Salford, an area which had a huge population (approximately 180,000 in 1838) but which was not represented in Parliament until the Reform Act of 1832. Giving the vote to women was not considered seriously during this period; indeed, they were only given the vote in 1926, and that was only for those over the age of 30.

In the 1790s, during the French Revolution, the need for reform was debated in Corresponding Societies, formed throughout Britain to educate labouring-class people about their rights, and in the radical press. The *Political Register*, a weekly newspaper written by William Cobbett, attacked what he called 'Old Corruption' in the political system. His targets were government sinecures, posts which held titles and wages but which involved little or no actual work, the payment of government pensions, overtaxation and the national debt. He was part of a radical reform movement that also involved debating societies, publishing pamphlets, massive petitions to Government, open-air meetings, marches and peaceful demonstrations. In periods of such activity, the Government clamped down on radicals, issuing the so-called 'Gagging Acts' in 1795 and the 'six acts' in 1819. Habeas Corpus, the right that anyone who is imprisoned has to a trial, was suspended twice during the Romantic period, in 1795 and again in 1817, both years noted for bad harvests, economic distress and civil unrest. There were some achievements for the reform movement:

when members of the London Corresponding Society and the Society for Constitutional Information were tried for High Treason in 1794, they were all acquitted.

The Prince Regent, who came to power in 1811 following his father's degeneration into illness, aroused much criticism from the radical press for his luxurious lifestyle and extravagances, which incurred huge debts that had to be paid for by Parliament raising his allowance in 1796 and again in 1803. When he tried in 1820 to stop his legal wife, Caroline of Brunswick, from being crowned Queen by putting her on trial for adultery, the British public rose up in her defence (he had secretly and illegally married a Catholic woman, Maria Fitzherbert, in 1785). Where the Prince Regent's carriage had been mobbed and missiles thrown at it in January 1817, Caroline's journey to London in June 1820 was accompanied by throngs of supporters.

In 1819 the 'Gagging Acts' were extended and added to, with the 'six acts' brought in to repress another flare-up of radical activity. The Blasphemous and Seditious Libels Act was particularly worrying for political writers and publishers who lived in constant fear of imprisonment and trial, with the sentence increased to transportation for 14 years. In response to spies' tales of ordinary people arming themselves and practising army-style drilling and marching, the Government passed the Training Prevention Act and the Seizure of Arms Act. They also prohibited meetings of more than 50 people. One of the defining events of the Romantic period took place on St Peter's Field in Manchester on 16 August 1819, and was dubbed the 'Peterloo massacre' with obvious ironic reference to the Battle of Waterloo four years earlier. This meeting was an open-air demonstration and call for parliamentary reform, attended by around 60,000 men, women and children, who had gathered to listen to Henry Hunt, a radical orator and political activist. The mere presence of women and children was considered as proof that the demonstration was a peaceful protest but local magistrates ordered the crowd to be forcibly dispersed, killing at least ten people and injuring hundreds more. The dispersal was particularly vicious, with the local yeomanry, made up of shopkeepers and manufacturers pursuing personal vendettas, seeking out the flags of societies they knew from among the crowd and using their sabres from horseback on unarmed people. After Peterloo, the Home Secretary, Lord Sidmouth, sent his congratulations and thanks to the magistrates for their actions. In 'England in 1819', the poet Shelley lamented, 'A people starved and stabbed in th'untilled field', ruled by 'An old mad, blind, despised, and dying King' and his sons, 'Princes, the dregs of their dull race, who flow / Through public scorn' (Norton 2006, vol. 2: 771). He must have despaired of reform ever being achieved, and indeed it was not to come for more than a decade after these events.

PHILOSOPHY AND RELIGION

This section considers the influence that Enlightenment philosophy exerted on the Romantic period, paying particular attention to the work of John Locke, David Hume, David Hartley. The section goes on to look at the idealist philosophy of Bishop Berkeley and the transcendentalism of Immanuel Kant that influenced Coleridge, among other writers. In its discussion of the period's religion, this section discusses the pantheism seen in the early careers of Wordsworth and Coleridge, Thomas Paine's deism, Percy Shelley's atheism, Godwin's Unitarian background, and John Wesley's Methodism as examples of the many faiths practised and rejected during these times. The huge church building project undergone in this period offers an example of both the anxieties and orthodoxies of religious belief in an age that saw the Gordon Riots against the Catholic Relief Acts and, eventually, the Repeal of the Test and Corporations Act (1828).

Natural Theology

Religious faith was attacked on many different grounds during the Romantic period, from scientific, political and

philosophical perspectives. The French Revolution created a
secular state, one that would no longer recognize the authority of the king or the clergy. Earlier in the century the French
surgeon, Julian Offray de la Mettrie, had written a book
called *L'Homme Machine, or, The Machine Man* (1747), which
argued that human beings could be regarded as machines,
and that their behaviour might be explained as conforming
to certain predictable rules and laws. La Mettrie's idea did
not allow for an immortal or spiritual part of man; the soul,
if it existed, would, he believed, be seen by physicians when
they operated on the body (de la Mettrie 1996: 4–5). It
seemed to some, after Newton's discovery of the law of
gravity, that the world was a machine which worked mechan-
ically according to regular and universal rules that could
be discovered and explained by scientists. This, of course,
begged the question of whether there was any need to
imagine a God, when the world seemed to work like clock-
work without need of a governing or directing force.

The analogy with a clock was one that provided some with
an answer to such questions. William Paley in his popular
book *Natural Theology* (1802) considered the difference
between finding a watch or a stone on the ground:

> In crossing a heath, suppose I pitched my foot against a *stone* and
> were asked how the stone came to be there, I might possibly
> answer that for anything I knew to the contrary it had lain there
> forever [. . .] But suppose I had found a *watch* upon the ground,
> and it should be inquired how the watch happened to be in that
> place, I should hardly think of the answer which I had before
> given [. . .] [because] when we come to inspect the watch we
> perceive – what we could not discover in the stone – that its
> several parts are framed and put together for a purpose. (Paley
> 1802: 1)

The difference between the watch and the stone is that the
watch clearly appears to have been 'designed' by someone,
and Paley goes on to argue that there is other, equally clear
evidence of design in the natural world; in, for example, the

eye of a fish or the operation of the lungs of animals. He was countering the opinions of followers of the Scottish Enlightenment philosopher, David Hume, who denied that there was any need to believe in a First Cause, a someone or something who had designed, constructed and set the world going. The only reason that we think there must be, Hume argued, was that we were accustomed to thinking that every effect had a cause, which in fact was a matter of habit; it was simply something we expected rather than anything we could prove.

The Enlightenment, materialism and transcendentalism

The period immediately preceding the Romantic era is known as the Enlightenment, and the Romantic emphasis on imagination is often positioned against the Enlightenment's emphasis on reason. Rather than being primarily concerned with the rational, the Romantic period was fascinated with the irrational, the superstitious and mysterious; with madness, with feelings and with the imagination. There was a reaction against what the scientist Humphry Davy called in his 1830 *Consolations in Travel* the 'dull, cold, heavy doctrine' of materialism held by the French, something he believed was 'necessarily tending to atheism' (Davy cited by Knight 1992: 179). In the Romantic period the philosophy of Immanuel Kant, a German idealist who believed that there was something more real than mere matter, was influential. His philosophy has become known as transcendentalism and argues that there is something beyond the material world, beyond that which is actually tangible. While reason might govern our knowledge and experience of the material world, Kant pointed out that we also are capable of moral reasoning, of making choices because they are the right or the dutiful choices to make. The question of how well known Kant's philosophy was in Britain is a vexed one, but it was certainly known to Coleridge, who studied the German philosophers.

However, much Enlightenment philosophy continued to influence Romantic thinking. John Locke in Britain, another key figure of the Enlightenment, emphasized the importance of 'empiricism', a belief in the world we can see and touch, or, in other words, that we can experience. Coleridge himself had first been influenced by David Hartley, whose *Observations on Man* (1749) took its cue from Locke's idea that people were not born with innate ideas. Locke imagined people as a kind of blank canvas or *tabula rasa*. The monster in *Frankenstein* (1818) by Mary Shelley (1797–1851) is imagined this way, as his first impressions of the world and its inhabitants are experienced with a kind of innocence and openness. Hartley believed that sensations were physical vibrations in the nerves; moral awareness was achieved by reflecting on these sensations. This idea of a solitary and personal reflection on one's experiences of the empirical world particularly appealed to Wordsworth, whose early poetry is filled with such moments of internal exploration: 'emotion recollected in tranquillity' (Norton 2006, vol. 2: 273). Believing that we are not born with innate ideas places a much greater emphasis on the importance of our environment. In other words, it is the way that the monster in *Frankenstein* is treated that creates his desire for revenge and murder rather than that he is simply evil. This philosophical emphasis on environment as the most important influence on character and happiness led to an interest in children and education that persisted throughout the Romantic period. Jean-Jacques Rousseau's influence is apparent here; his educational treatise *Emile* (1762) encouraged raising children in a more natural way and allowing them to develop at their own pace, based on a belief that people are naturally good but that society and civilization corrupt them. Rousseau's ideas influenced the early radical Romantics greatly, helping Wollstonecraft to formulate her ideas on the way that 'females [. . .] are made women of' (Wollstonecraft 1997: 245–6). She was angered, though, by Rousseau's refusal to see in women the same potential as he saw in men, and in her *A Vindication of the Rights of Woman* (1792) outlined the way that environment or society constructed and corrupted female identities.

Wordsworth's and Coleridge's confidence in Hartley's ideas waned but not before Coleridge had named his first child after the philosopher. The problem they had with Hartley was that he perceived the mind as a passive tool, merely receiving impressions from the world. For the Romantics the mind was essentially active and creative; Wordsworth could see that memory was only partly recollection and that the imagination was also at work in the exercise of remembering childhood. For him the senses 'half create' what they perceive ('Lines. Composed a Few Miles above Tintern Abbey', Norton 2006, vol. 2: 260). This emphasis on the mind, and on individual subjectivity, was due partly to the influence of another philosopher, Bishop George Berkeley, who could not think of the mind as - material or inert but instead believed '*Esse est percipi*' or 'to be is to be perceived'. In other words, the external world has no independent existence from the mind that witnesses it. This idealism elevated the individual and subjectivity, or the ego.

This elevation of the ego can be seen in Coleridge's declaration that he had a 'smack of Hamlet' himself when he read Shakespeare's play, finding in the character a reflection of his own troubled psyche. In his poem 'Dejection: An Ode', Coleridge's unrequited love for an unattainable woman, his unhappy marriage, and a belief in the superior poetic powers of his friend Wordsworth combine to make him incapable of feeling the beauty of nature. The poem is introspective, and again the cause of the problem is internal: he 'may not hope from outward forms to win / The passion and the life, whose fountains are within' (Norton 2006, vol. 2: 467). Coleridge's theory of the imagination, set out in his *Biographia Literaria* (1817), countered the idea of the world as a lifeless machine. He described the imagination as 'the living power and prime agent of all human perception' (Norton 2006, vol. 2: 477). Percy Shelley wrote in *Prometheus Unbound* that the poet, after watching the external world for a long time, can create 'Forms

more real than living man, / Nurslings of immortality!',
suggesting that the imagination can attain a greater 'truth' or
'reality' than the empirical world (Wu 2006: 1115–16).

As this section has so far suggested, Romanticism did not
diverge as strongly from Enlightenment philosophy as has
sometimes been suggested. The Scottish Enlightenment,
which was so important for the Romantics, was similar in
many respects to the larger movement, particularly in its
insistence that society was progressing and becoming more
civilized and polite. The ways in which these movement did
differ, though, can be explained by the political events that
influenced the Scottish one, specifically the loss of independence caused by Scotland's Union with England. Prominent
figures in the Scottish Enlightenment were Frances
Hutcheson, David Hume, Thomas Reid, Adam Smith and
Dugald Stewart. Edinburgh was the focus of this movement,
with its impressive university still regarded as providing an
excellent education in law, economics, medicine and mathe-
matics. A general resistance to universal or transcendental
explanations of human morals and behaviour encouraged
an interest in history during the Romantic period, which
became especially apparent in the work produced in
Scotland at this time. Scottish writers, Walter Scott
(1771–1832) being the most obvious example, wrote with a
particularly acute sense of historical self-awareness with
regard to Scotland's former political independence. Such
concerns were part of a larger shift in thought: the idea that
who we are is determined by our environment, by where and
when we live.

Religion in England, Ireland, Scotland and Wales

The majority of the population in England during this period
belonged to the Anglican Church of England, but in the
other countries of Britain there was quite a different picture.
Ireland was largely Roman Catholic presided over and ruled
by the representatives of the Church of England who
demanded taxes but were often absentee landlords, preferring

to remain in England. Lady Morgan, who wrote under the pen-name Sydney Owenson, campaigned for Catholic Emancipation. Her novel *The Wild Irish Girl* (1806) ended with the marriage of the son of an English landlord to the daughter of a deposed Irish king, which obviously symbolized the greater understanding and sympathy that could exist between the Catholic and Protestant populations of Ireland and England. Catholics were disenfranchised, denied the vote or any participation in politics, and attempts to make life and worship easier for Catholics in the form of the Catholic Relief Acts of 1778 and 1791 caused much turmoil. These acts made it possible for Catholics to buy new property, to join the army, swear allegiance to the king without having to renounce their beliefs, and their priests were no longer considered to be committing a felony.

Such measures of toleration towards the Catholics provoked the worst riots on British soil during the Romantic period – the so-called Gordon Riots in London – which lasted 2–10 June 1780. They were named after Lord George Gordon, who objected to the first of the Catholic Relief Acts, which was really an attempt to win the support of Scottish and Irish Catholics in the American Revolution. The poet and engraver William Blake (1757–1827) was among the first wave of attackers on Newgate Prison, which was burned down along with other buildings. Houses were damaged, Catholic chapels were burned, and mob risings also took place in Bristol and other provincial towns. The Catholic question was a live one throughout this entire period: both William Pitt the Younger and George Grenville resigned as prime minister in 1801 and 1807 respectively when King George III refused to allow any further measures towards Catholic emancipation, and when on the throne, his son, George IV, continued to refuse royal support. In spite of this, there were major victories for the Catholics, and in the 1820s Daniel O'Connell mobilized the Catholic clergy, resulting in his being elected as an MP for County Clare even though he was not permitted to take office because he was Catholic. Eventually bowing to the pressure of forces in Ireland, the

Roman Catholic Relief Act was passed in 1829, which allowed Catholics to sit in Parliament.

Scotland was divided in its religion between north and south, though both were governed by the Presbyterian Church of Scotland, whose existence had been guaranteed by the Act of Union (1707). This act had firmly brought England and Scotland together as the Kingdom of Great Britain. Many in the Highlands of Scotland were Catholics, but elsewhere the Scottish religion was predominantly Calvinist, harking back to the Scottish Reformation, which had occurred independently of the English one. This sect was founded on a more severe idea than English Protestantism, namely the Calvinist doctrine of predestination, which held not only that had God decided which of his elect would be saved but also that all others would be damned.

In Wales there were many more Non-Conformists than Anglicans, and again nationalism contributed to a religious identity that was distinctive from that of England, Ireland or Scotland. The number of chapels built during this period in Wales testifies to the success of the Dissenting (see **Dissenters**) religions. One of these sects, Methodism, was very popular in Wales, though it had originated in England with John Wesley. Wesley and his supporters responded to the apathy they found with enthusiastic fire-and-brimstone sermons, preaching in the open air to factory workers or the rural poor, like the lecture given by Dinah Morris in George Eliot's *Adam Bede*, which, though published in 1859, was set in Yorkshire, in the north of England, around the year 1800.

During this period England suffered from a general apathy regarding religion, with church attendance at what was considered an alarmingly low rate. This was particularly the case in the new industrial towns and the highly populated city of London. The capital was growing at a fast pace and, indifference apart, simply did not have enough amenities and churches for the number of people to which it was now home. The huge church building project costing one million pounds of public funds that was undertaken by Lord Liverpool's Government does not appear to have effected much increase in church-going during the period, and at a time where some of the population were actually starving, Liverpool's project did little to help raise the reputation of organized religion in the minds of many.

Dissenting Traditions: Rationalism and Utopianism

William Godwin's *Enquiry into Political Justice* (1793) contains an optimism and a belief in rationalism that is owed partly to Enlightenment philosophy, which had a similar conviction that the world was progressing. His treatise emphasized the way that political institutions shaped and moulded the individual minds and characters of subjects. In the Preface to his fictional version of *Political Justice*, the novel *Caleb Williams* (1794), he wrote: 'It is now known to philosophers that the spirit and character of the government intrudes itself into every rank of society' (Godwin 1982: 1). He intended, with the story of Caleb Williams, 'to comprehend, as far as the progressive nature of a single story would allow, a general review of the modes of domestic and unrecorded despotism by which man becomes the destroyer of man' (Godwin 1982: 1). It is important to remember that in the Romantic period the Established Church was, of course, one of the political institutions to which Godwin was referring.

Godwin's utopianism was also partly the result of his religious beliefs; he had been raised a Dissenter, and had intended to join the ministry. He graduated from the Hoxton Dissenting Academy, set up to educate those who were not allowed a university education because of their religious beliefs, in an area of London well known for its community of like-minded individuals. Although the majority of people in England were members of the Church of England, Protestants whose ascendancy was secured by the political machinations of sixteenth- and seventeenth-century monarchs and governments, there was a small portion of men and women who, though Protestant, had moved away from the Church of England in a variety of ways and these were lumped together under the title of Dissenters. The Test and

Corporation Acts, passed in the seventeenth century, made it impossible for Dissenters to hold civil or military public office. Unitarians, one specific group of Dissenters, rejected the Trinity, believing either that Jesus was of a lesser order than God, or that he was human rather than divine. During the Romantic period, Dissenters, particularly Unitarians, often held important roles in literary, political, scientific and religious arenas. They tended to be from the educated middle classes, were politically liberal, and were pushing for parliamentary reform and religious toleration. Dr Richard Price, for example, a Dissenting minister in Stoke Newington, London, famously expressed support for the revolution in France in 1789 when he likened it to England's 'Glorious Revolution' of 1688. The backlash to such sentiments can be seen in the burning of the house and laboratory of another famous dissenter, Joseph Priestley, after he took part in celebrations for the anniversary of the French Revolution in 1791. Priestley lost most of his manuscripts, library and equipment and was eventually forced to leave England. Price and Priestley shared, with the young Coleridge, a millennial optimism (see **Millenarianism**), convinced that the Second Coming of Christ would soon take place. The events of the French Revolution seemed to suggest that dramatic change was imminent, and was often represented as an apocalyptic event which would be followed by a thousand years of Christ's rule before the end of the world at the Last Judgement. Further along the spectrum from the respectable positions held by rational Dissenters were prophets such as Joanna Southcott. She was a domestic servant who published her prophecies and toured Britain, gaining supporters. At the end of her life, aged 63, she declared that she was pregnant with Christ's child, to be named Shiloh, but despite her pregnancy being confirmed by a number of London surgeons, no child arrived.

The position of a Dissenter in Britain is described by Anna Barbauld in her poem 'A Mouse's Petition' (1773), written as though by a mouse awaiting probable death in one of Priestley's experiments on air. The mouse appeals to his captor for his release on the grounds that he is 'a free-born mouse' and one of 'nature's commoners', pointing out that he breathes the same air as Priestley, drinks the same water, and that these are 'The common gifts of heaven' (Barbauld 1773: 38, 39). The mouse appeals to Priestley as a Unitarian, as one within whose breast freedom glows; there is clearly a sense that Priestley, having encountered such treatment himself, should help others whom tyrants oppress. The poem is partly an in-joke, a mock petition, which is a form usually used to make demands of governments or monarchs. During this period, some people were increasingly unhappy at the way that animals were being treated in scientific experiments, and, on the surface, it seems to be a poem arguing against cruelty to animals. But the fact that this poem is written by a woman whose religious beliefs are Non-Conformist is surely significant. Barbauld is refused political rights (the right to vote, to hold government office, to go to university) on two counts: firstly because she is a woman and secondly because she is a Dissenter. She holds, as Marlon Ross has put it, a position of 'double-dissent' (Ross 1993: 92). It is testament to the changed mood at the end of the Romantic period that the Test and Corporations Act was repealed in 1828.

Pantheism, deism and atheism

The young Wordsworth and Coleridge described in their poetry pantheistic (see **Pantheism**) religious sentiments which have come to symbolize a peculiarly Romantic idea of nature. Coleridge describes these sentiments in his poem 'The Eolian Harp' (1796; 1817):

> O! the one Life within us and abroad,
> Which meets all motion and becomes its soul,
> A light in sound, a sound-like power in light,
> Rhythm in thought, and joyance everywhere –
> Methinks, it should have been impossible
> Not to love all things in a world so filled;
> [. . .]

And what if all of animated nature
Be but organic harps diversely framed,
That tremble into thought, as o'er them sweeps
Plastic and vast, one intellectual breeze,
At once the Soul of each, and God of All?

(Norton 2006, vol. 2: 427)

Coleridge here finds God in nature and in everything, and imagines that we all partake of the life of God. He uses the analogy of an Aeolian harp, which was an instrument that lay lengthwise across the sill of an open window. As the breeze blew in through the window, it would cause the harp's strings to vibrate and make a sound. This is an analogy in the poem for all of 'animated nature', with God being the 'intellectual breeze' that inspires us all. Of course, in Coleridge's case, the harp is a symbol of the poet who is inspired by God, who is in nature, to write.

Another form of 'natural religion' was made popular in Europe and America by the revolutionary deist writer, Thomas Paine, in *The Age of Reason* (1794). Deists believed that God created the world but does not intervene in it, so while he can be seen in the beauty of nature there is no need to believe in miracles or revelation. Here, again, the influence of Newton and other scientific discoveries can be felt; deism insisted upon reason rather than faith as the only grounds upon which to believe in God. Such sentiments combined in Paine with a conviction that all things should be equal. Many of the first presidents and politicians of the US, including Thomas Jefferson and Benjamin Franklin, were deists.

It is easy to see why natural religions, such as deism and pantheism, were treated with suspicion and distrust by the Established Church in Britain at this time; both Wordsworth and Coleridge, as they became more conservative in their political beliefs also became more orthodox in their religion. Many in this period thought that natural religion was tantamount to atheism, but then there were also those not afraid to call themselves atheists, though it cost them dear. An atheist does not believe in God, and it was dangerous in those times to declare that you held such beliefs. Percy Shelley had been expelled from Oxford for writing, with his friend, a pamphlet called *The Necessity of Atheism* (1811), which they had sent to bishops across Britain. Later in his life, he was refused custody of his two children by his first wife because of the blasphemous sentiment contained in his poem *Queen Mab* (1813). After his death by drowning in 1822, one particularly callous obituary writer wrote in one newspaper that 'Shelley, the writer of some infidel poetry, has been drowned; *now* he knows whether there is a God or no' (cited by Bieri 2005: 338).

When the Blasphemy Act of 1698 was joined by the Blasphemous and Seditious Libels Act of 1819 it became even more dangerous for writers to print atheist or free-thinking ideas. Richard Carlile was fined and imprisoned for republishing Paine's *Age of Reason* and Elihu Palmer's *Principles of Nature* (1801), and during his career his wife and sister were also imprisoned for helping publish such work. The Society for the Suppression of Vice was set up to guard society's morals, publicly burning books and passing the names of authors, publishers and booksellers on to government officials to enable their arrest. These were dangerous times in which to live if you did not conform to established religious and political beliefs.

SCIENCE AND TECHNOLOGY

This section argues for the centrality of science, as much as any other aspect of culture, to Romanticism. The new technologies of the period were hugely exciting, from the steam engine to the hot-air balloon travel, new printing technology and industrialization. Natural history, chemistry, geology, electricity and optics were all popular sciences in this period, as Humphry Davy's lectures at the Royal Institution testify, while this period also saw the increased professionalization of science. Finally, the debate on the nature of life between surgeons John Abernethy and William Lawrence, in which religious beliefs reasserted their authority on matters of the soul and the mind, gives us an insight into the materialist tendencies of writers such as Percy Shelley.

The Romantic period saw the emergence of many disciplines that we would now incorporate within the term 'science'. Before, this word had been used to mean knowledge in a general sense, and it was not until a meeting of the British Association for the Advancement of Science in 1833 that the poet Coleridge proposed the use of the word 'science' as an equivalent term to 'artist' (Anon. 1834: 59). Previously the phrases 'man of science' and 'natural philosopher' were far more common. The coining of this new term is indicative of the organization and professionalism of science during this period, as disciplines became more carefully defined and science moved from the homes and makeshift laboratories of men in the provinces to become government-supported activities, often reflecting the interests of the landed gentry or the concerns of an imperialist power.

This was a period which saw the setting up of formal institutions and societies such as the Geological Society (1807), the Royal Institution (1799), the Linnaean Society (1788), and the Royal Astronomical Society (1820). It was also the age of the museum, and the British Museum (founded in 1753) had acquired collections of plants, fossils and other natural history specimens, while there were often shows of rare and exotic animals in London. Before his death, one surgeon, John Hunter, amassed a huge collection of unusual skeletons, diseased body-parts and deformities which now belongs to the Royal College of Surgeons. There were many important scientific inventions made during this period. The astronomer Sir William Herschel discovered the planet Uranus in 1781, or, as it was originally called, *Georgium Sidus* (George's Star) in honour of the king. There were also significant medical advances, particularly the success of Edward Jenner's vaccination for smallpox. A number of major new engineering works and manufacturing inventions accompanied Britain's industrialization, including Thomas

Telford's suspension bridges, many of which still stand today. New canals and roads also improved transportation around the country.

Chemistry

Some of the most impressive advances during this period were made in chemistry, though the boundaries of this discipline were rather loosely defined and practitioners tended to be gentlemen of leisure rather than professionals in the sense that we would understand. The career of Humphry Davy, the foremost chemist of the period, traced the development of this science from the work of provincial radicals Joseph Priestley and Thomas Beddoes to the grand and politically conservative institutions of the Royal Institution and the Royal Society. Chemists made a number of important discoveries. 'Common' or atmospheric air was recognized as not being a single element but a compound: 'fixed air' (carbon), 'azote' (nitrogen) and 'pure air' (oxygen) were found to be present in air, and were examined for their respective vital properties. The work of the French chemist Antoine-Laurent Lavoisier, who was guillotined during the Terror in revolutionary France, was decisive in bringing about the 'chemical revolution' of this period. In 1783, he and Simon Pierre Laplace demonstrated that during respiration the different elements of air worked to different ends: oxygen burned the carbon in food, and the heat of this combustion produced 'animal heat' or the warmth animals needed to survive. This chemical process also formed carbon dioxide, which was emitted from the body during respiration.

In Britain, Priestley identified 20 new gases between 1770 and 1800, publishing five volumes describing his experiments. He also inadvertently discovered what we would now call photosynthesis, the need that animals and plants have for sunlight, but his reluctance to give up old-fashioned eighteenth-century ideas of 'imponderables', invisible and weightless fluids such as 'phlogiston', which he and others believed explained changes in temperature during heating, hindered his achievements. He refused to accept either that Lavoisier had done as he claimed to have done in separating decomposing water into its two composite parts of oxygen and hydrogen, or John Dalton's new theory of atoms. Priestley's main problem with Lavoisier concerned his inability to replicate his experiments; they had been performed using far more expensive equipment than the teacups and saucers used by Priestley. For Priestley, science was connected inextricably with politics and religion; his efforts were to rid the world of superstition and ignorance, and the philanthropic uses of his discoveries were always of primarily importance. As he wrote in *Experiments and Observations on Different Kinds of Air*: 'the English hierarchy (if there be anything unsound in its constitution) has equal reason to tremble even at an air pump, or an electrical machine' (cited by Golinski 1992: 81). Edmund Burke, speaking from a different political perspective, repeatedly used metaphors drawn from the study of gas in his *Reflections upon the Revolution in France*. Speaking of the need to be cautious in praising the Revolution, though no doubt implying a slur upon Priestley's radical politics and science, Burke wrote: 'The wild *gas*, the fixed air is plainly broke loose: but we ought to suspend our judgment until the first effervescence is a little subsided, till the liquor is cleared, and until we see something deeper than the agitation of a troubled and frothy surface' (Burke 1999: 417–18).

The natural world revealed by chemists of the early nineteenth century was one in which matter was not annihilated after death but was changed into another form. The same elements recombined to produce new compounds. Broadly, chemistry concerned itself with the movement between different states. As John Dalton wrote in his seminal *New System of Chemical Philosophy*:

> Chemical analysis and synthesis go no further than to the separation of particles one from another, and to their reunion. No new creation or destruction of matter is within the reach of chemical agency. We might as well attempt to introduce a new planet into the solar system, or to annihilate one already in

existence, as to create or destroy a particle of hydrogen. (Dalton 1808, vol. 1: 212)

Dalton argues here that a limited number of single particles of each element exist in the world, and while they may continue to combine and recombine in an infinite variety of forms, they will never cease to exist. Dalton presents a world which has a deliberate and recognizable system where each component is used to complement and benefit the others. Dalton's and Priestley's science imagined a world that was harmonious, with a divinely ordained system in which no element has been created without purpose and each has its mutually beneficial role.

The Lunar Society

Both Priestley and Dalton belonged to provincial scientific circles, Priestley being a member of the Lunar Society, an extraordinary group of men who lived in the Midlands and met once a month around the time of the full moon to talk about scientific matters. This group included Matthew Boulton, an industrialist; Erasmus Darwin, the grandfather of Charles Darwin; Thomas Day, the author of the children's novel *History of Sandford and Merton* (1783–9); Richard Lovell Edgeworth, father of Maria Edgeworth; James Watt, an engineer; and Josiah Wedgwood, a potter and Charles Darwin's maternal grandfather. Erasmus Darwin not only had a medical practice in his home town of Lichfield but also invented such things as a mechanical speaking head and a writing-copying machine. He had a huge range of interests, as was common in an eighteenth-century natural philosopher, and disseminated scientific knowledge in poems that were accompanied by copious notes. His *The Loves of the Plants* (1789) largely concerned the sexual system of plants that Swedish botanist, Carl Linnaeus, had set out, and which Darwin had earlier translated, attempting to use frank, direct language rather than the euphemisms of other versions. The topic was a controversial one since Linnaeus classified plants by the reproductive organs, the stamen (male) or pistil (female), and as a result botany was regarded as a discipline that was inappropriate for women to study. The discovery of sexual organs in plants, though, encouraged a sense that there were more similarities between plant and animal life than had previously been recognized; Darwin's poems personified plants and what he called the 'vegetable passion of love' (Darwin 1791: 197).

Such beliefs could easily be interpreted as the scientific basis on which to found characteristically 'Romantic' or pantheistic concepts of a living, breathing world. Instead of a dead, inert Newtonian universe, the world is seen as a dynamic play of forces, where attraction and repulsion are analogous to the human emotions of love and hate, and where the natural world (the nightingale for Keats, the skylark for Shelley, and the daffodil for Wordsworth) can provoke a sympathetic, emotional response in us. Though containing what many considered to be salacious and erotic material unsuited to female readers, Darwin's poems are lengthy and written in heroic-verse couplets that fit an earlier eighteenth-century literary tradition rather than a Romantic one. However, he influenced many Romantic authors, from Wordsworth's tale of 'Goody Blake and Harry Gill' in *Lyrical Ballads* (1798), to Mary Shelley's claim that *Frankenstein* was inspired by reports she had heard of the 'experiments of Dr Darwin [. . .] who preserved a piece of vermicelli in a glass case, till by some extraordinary means it began to move with a voluntary motion' (M. Shelley 1994: 364). Charles Darwin's early introduction to his grandfather's ideas, including the latter's speculation that all life had come from one single parent, and that life had first emerged from the seas, had obvious influence on his own theory of natural selection. Charles may also have learned caution from the reaction of conservative reviewers to Darwin's work; his *Temple of Nature* was regarded as 'glaringly Atheistical' and his reputation was seriously damaged (Anon. 1809: 120).

The Lunar Society differed from other societies in London, such as the Royal Society, in its interest in industrialization rather than in technology that would aid agricultural development for the landed gentry. Many of the inventions and patents registered by Lunar Society members were to help develop the technology used in factories such as the Soho Manufactory owned by Boulton and Watt near Birmingham, and the Wedgwood potteries, called Etruria, in Stoke-on-Trent. Watt made significant improvements in the steam engine, and patented a new engine which was less wasteful in its consumption of fuel. He also introduced the use of 'horsepower' as a unit to measure power in steam engines.

Matthew Boulton was a highly successful businessman who transformed his father's shoe and breeches buckle-making business, eventually producing a wide range of steel, ceramic and enamel objects, including plate (flat sheets of metal) and minting new copper coins in the Soho Mint, while the Soho Foundry used innovative techniques that reflected Boulton's interest in metallurgy. The house that Boulton had built at Soho for himself featured many of the inventions of his fellow 'lunaticks', including a central-heating system that was probably the first seen in Britain since Roman times. Boulton was also, with other Lunar Society members, interested in the potential presented by hot-air balloons, which had first been launched by the Mongolfier brothers in France in 1783. These were described by Anna Barbauld in 'Washing Day' as something she could not have imagined when she was a child: 'little dreaming then / To see, Mongolfier, thy silken ball / Ride buoyant through the clouds' (Norton 2006, vol. 2: 38).

While many of Boulton's enterprises were for a mass market, he also attempted to integrate his products into the luxury market, though with far less commercial success. Josiah Wedgwood similarly moved from an early business in mass-produced tableware to ornamental vases and cameos made for aristocratic and royal customers. He had a London showroom and was Queen Caroline's official potter. Wedgwood also made considerable advances in pottery methods, using innovative techniques involving equipment more usually found in the metal industry. Both Boulton and

Wedgwood showed consideration for their workers, with Boulton setting up a friendly society for his factory workers and Wedgwood contributing to a sick-benefit scheme for his. This contrasted sharply with conditions experienced in the factories in overpopulated cities such as Manchester. Wedgwood was a Unitarian and was involved in the anti-slavery movement, producing a medallion that showed a kneeling slave in chains and inscribed with the words: 'Am I not a man and a brother?' His son, Thomas Wedgwood, upon inheriting his father's fortune, was able to give financial help to others and paid Coleridge an annual income. He also made some early experiments in photography. Due to his failing health, he consulted Thomas Beddoes, the son-in-law of Lunar Society member Richard Lovell Edgeworth, and gave £1,000 towards a 'Pneumatic Institution', which tested whether gases, particularly nitrous oxide, were useful for medical purposes. James Watt's son, Gregory, was treated there in the hope that nitrous oxide could help his consumption, and the chemist Humphry Davy held his first job there as Beddoes' assistant.

From Provincial Science to the Royal Society

Beddoes was also a radical in his politics. He had been forced to resign his readership at the University of Oxford because of his public support of the French Revolution and his equally public criticism of Pitt's Government. Beddoes probably first met Coleridge on a demonstration against the 'Gagging Acts' in 1795. Robert Southey and Peter Mark Roget, the author of the *Thesaurus* (1852), were also in Beddoes' circle at this time, and when Davy began experimenting with nitrous oxide they joined him, proclaiming that the gas was a kind of truth-seeing drug. Davy, after a particularly heavy dose, reported: 'nothing exists but thoughts' (Davy 1800: 489). His politics clearly matched those of his companions at this time: in the notebooks he kept in the 1790s, the young Davy is a republican in his politics and a materialist in his science, describing Britain as 'a mighty

Nation groaning under the Chains of Tyranny & sustaining the pang of Oppression' (cited by Ruston 2005: 36). In his first publication, part of Beddoes' and Watts' 1799 *Contributions to Physical and Medical Knowledge*, Davy disputed Lavoisier's analysis of oxygen, instead claiming that oxygen should more properly be called 'phosoxygen', thereby claiming that light was also present (Davy 1799). A 1799 review of this essay in *The British Critic*, while allowing that the idea was 'ingenious', described it as 'leading to materialism' and therefore 'highly objectionable' (Anon. 1799: 627). After having his fingers burned by this first publishing attempt, Davy was very careful never to publish anything that could be construed as materialist again, protecting his reputation fiercely. Indeed, when he moved to join the Royal Institution in London in 1800, he began to disassociate himself from Beddoes, Priestley and Godwin and their radical circles. In London, he came under the influence of Sir Joseph Banks, the President of the Royal Society between 1778 and 1820, who vetted any attempts to create other scientific societies than those that already existed.

Banks' own house, 32 Soho Square in London, was itself described as the 'perfect museum', its rooms full of exotic items that Banks had collected on his travels with Captain Cook's ship the *Endeavour* in 1768 and which his extensive network of scientific contacts across the world had sent him (Fulford, Lee and Kitson 2004: 41). Rooms contained 'thousands of dried plants preserved in purpose-designed cases and painstakingly catalogued'. His natural history library contained at least 22,000 items, including maps and accounts of journeys to remote places. Banks was a personal friend of the king and in 1773 was appointed to direct Kew Gardens, where 'he cultivated seedlings from around the world – increasing the species held from 3,400 to 11,000' (Fulford, Lee and Kitson 2004: 41). His objective for science was always to benefit landowners and to further the nation's imperialist agenda. He was openly hostile to the provincial networks of Priestley and Beddoes, refusing to support their projects, and after his move to London, Davy did the same.

Southey wrote to a mutual friend in 1804: 'You never mention Davy, alias the Galvanic Spark, and I never think of the baneful effects of prosperity without remembering him' (Southey 1965, vol. 1: 358). At the end of his life, as President of the Royal Society himself, Davy became increasingly reactionary, nationalistic and conservative, playing an important role in the removal of science from the egalitarian, philanthropic and inexpensive experiments of Priestley, Beddoes and the Lunar Society to the institutionalized science of London's metropolitan centre.

The science of Frankenstein

Davy's lectures to the Royal Institution were well attended and did much to disseminate knowledge of chemistry to the middle classes and women. It seems likely that Professor Waldman, Victor Frankenstein's tutor and mentor in Mary Shelley's *Frankenstein*, is modelled on Davy, since there are similarities between Waldman's fictional lectures and Davy's 1802 lectures which Mary Shelley read (Crouch 1978). *Frankenstein* offers a critique of modern science; set in the 1790s it shows us Mary Shelley's perception of science, its greatest wonders and achievements, and its potential dangers. Anne Mellor has argued that *Frankenstein* is primarily a dramatized conflict between two camps: 'that scientific research which attempts to describe accurately the functionings of the physical universe and that which attempts to *control* or *change* the universe through human intervention' (Mellor 1988: 90). Mellor sees the first type of scientist, celebrated by Mary Shelley, as epitomized by the work of Erasmus Darwin, but the second, dangerous type of scientist as represented by Davy, or by an Italian called Luigi Galvani (Mellor 1988: 90).

The image of the scientist as a crazed inventor, working alone without considering the consequences of his discoveries for society at large has been perpetuated by the many film versions of the *Frankenstein* story. The suggestion made in Mary Shelley's novel that electricity would 'infuse a spark of being' into lifeless bodies and make them live again was one circulating in the work of Galvani and others at the time (M. Shelley 1994: 85). As Mary Shelley wrote in an 1831 Introduction to her book, 'galvanism had given token of such things' (M. Shelley 1994: 364). Great advances had been made in the science since 1750 when Benjamin Franklin discovered that lightning was static electricity. Franklin invented a kite that could harness this power, bringing it down from the sky to be used for domestic purposes. In the 1780s, Galvani experimented with frogs' legs stripped to the nerves and spinal chord. He tried attaching these to an electrical machine, or Leyden Jar, and to an insulated wire that reached into the air outside his house during a storm. In both cases he witnessed a response from the animal remains: in the second experiment, 'as often as the lightning broke out, at the same moment of time all the muscles fell into violent and multiple contractions' (Galvani 1953: 36). The most sensational experiments, though, were those performed by Galvani's nephew, Giovanni Aldini. He visited London, performing experiments on the bodies of criminals who had been cut down from the gallows on which they had just been hanged for their crimes. Aldini reported that the corpses he electrified seemed to be attempting to stand or sit up, they opened their eyes, clenched their fists, raised their arms and beat their hands violently against the table. Observers ran screaming from the room.

Those hanged for murder provided the only bodies that anatomists were allowed to dissect, and this worked as an extra punishment for their crime until the Anatomy Act of 1832 was passed, which allowed for the corpses of the poor to be dissected if their relatives were not able to claim their bodies within a specified time. Given the inadequacy and expense of communications and transport at this time, it is unsurprising that the bill was so unpopular. To the religious, dissection had worrying implications for the soul and resurrection at Judgement Day. Before the bill, surgeons had paid grave-robbers, or 'resurrection men', to provide them with bodies and the public fear of grave-robbing was such that there were instances of the rich paying guards to stand watch over their graves after their funeral. In 1827, William Burke and William Hare took grave-robbing to its logical conclusion, with Burke being hanged and publicly dissected for killing the people whose bodies he then sold to a surgeon, Robert Knox, in Edinburgh.

The British people were also both heartened and scared by advances in resuscitation techniques; the efforts of the Humane Society, which had been founded in 1774, were much publicized in its pamphlets advising how to resuscitate persons drowned, or the 'apparently dead'. The society placed drags and other equipment at such sites as Hyde Park in London where people might be likely to fall into the Serpentine. Rescuers were rewarded with Humane Society medals, while those rescued were given Bibles and took part in processions through London. Mary Wollstonecraft was one of the many people 'saved' by the Humane Society's work, rescued and resuscitated after throwing herself off Putney Bridge in a suicide attempt in October 1795 (Williams 2001). The advances made in 'reanimating' victims of drowning, as it was then called, as well as reports of people waking up under the surgeon's knife, made people even more worried that they would be pronounced dead and buried prematurely; some coffins were fitted with bells so that in such cases help could be called.

The 'vitality debate'

An *Edinburgh Review* article published in 1814 asserted (sarcastically) that 'there is not, at this moment, a term which is used with greater ambiguity, than the term Life' (Anon. 1814: 386). The term 'death', too, was causing problems; the French *Encyclopédie* defined two kinds of death, 'incomplete' and 'absolute', claiming that the first kind could be 'cured' (Arasse 1989: 37). The Humane Society used the word 'resurrect' rather than resuscitate. Emerging from such redefinitions was a widely publicized debate on the nature of life between the London surgeons John Abernethy and William Lawrence, which took place in their lectures to the Royal College of Surgeons between 1814 and 1819. Indeed, Lawrence was the first person to use the word 'biology' in English, a science he defined as 'the science of life' (Lawrence 1819: 60). Abernethy was a respected teacher and surgeon at St Bartholomew's Hospital; he gave the first lecture to the college in 1814, which he claimed was based on the writings and conversation of the surgeon John Hunter. In this lecture, Abernethy put forward his theory of life: he did not believe that life depended on the organization of the body (its physical make-up) but that it existed as a material substance 'superadded' to the body, just like the soul. Lawrence had been Abernethy's protégé, but in lectures given to the same college he ridiculed his mentor's arguments, regarding them as old-fashioned. Lawrence had been influenced by the French materialists, and instead argued that life was simply the working operation of all the body's functions, the sum of its parts. These scientific discussions of life were exploited to support political and theological opinions and the conservative press and clergy united to condemn Lawrence, who they said was denying the existence of the soul. His defence that 'the theological doctrine of the soul, and its separate existence, has nothing to do with this physiological question' went unheard (Lawrence 1819: 8). Lawrence was suspended from his hospital posts and only allowed back when he had withdrawn the book and promised never to utter such sentiments again. After an 1823 pirate edition of the *Lectures* was published, Lawrence applied for copyright of his book. The Chancellor, Lord Eldon, refused it on the grounds that the material it contained was blasphemous, seditious and immoral.

This debate on the nature of life was another test case for the idea that science should be regarded as objective, and that religion should not be involved in scientific investigations; a battle that was to be fought with greater success with the publication of Charles Darwin's theory of evolution. Geologists of the Romantic period had similar problems trying to reconcile the new evidence they found of prehistoric ages with the Bible's account of creation. Fossil-hunting became a pastime among travellers and geology a fashionable pursuit. Some of the fossils that were found belonged to creatures which no longer existed on the planet, and such discoveries were only with some difficulty made to seem part of God's divine plan. One group, labelled the 'Neptunists', argued that fossils gave evidence that Noah's flood had occurred, the water having shaped the rock they could now see. But others saw clearly in such evidence that the earth had to be far older than the 6,000 years that the Bible claimed. James Hutton was denounced as an atheist when he wrote of the earth that 'we find no vestige of a beginning – no prospect of an end' (Hutton 1795, vol. 1: 200).

ARTS AND CULTURE

This section considers the peculiarly Romantic developments in art, particularly the '**picturesque**', and briefly looks at some of the most influential of British Romantic painters, Joseph Mallord William Turner, John Constable, Joshua Reynolds and Joseph Wright of Derby, while also considering other major genres in art, including the engravings of William Blake and the satirical cartoons of James Gillray and George Cruikshank. New technologies in printing and a wider literacy among the population encouraged the growth of a number of new newspapers and journals, promoting an interest in politics at home and abroad, and science and culture in general. This section also includes a discussion of the important explorations of Captain Cook in the South Seas, considering in more general terms the Romantics' interest in travel and travel writing. A continued British presence in the East, in India in particular, encouraged such societies as William Jones' Asiatic Society of Bengal to promote orientalist art and the notion of a shared cultural origin.

Painting

Many of the painters of the Romantic period had been the students of Joshua Reynolds at the Royal Academy, but when he died in 1792 the path was clear for innovations in landscape painting, as opposed to the historical paintings he had championed. There is a huge range in the styles and subjects of Romantic-era painters. Portraits remained popular, with Sir Thomas Lawrence chosen to paint the royal family, including a highly flattering picture of the by then rather corpulent *King George IV* (1814, National Portrait Gallery). Far from this traditional kind of painting, the Swiss-born Henri Fuseli painted psychologically disturbing pictures such as *The Nightmare* (1781, Goethe Museum) in which a hunched, grinning devil crouches on a sleeping woman. Fuseli was part of the publisher Joseph Johnson's circle in London in the 1790s and, for a time, the lover of Mary Wollstonecraft. He spent many years of his life painting subjects from John Milton's works, and established his Milton Gallery in 1799. Literature provided subjects for many other painters, too, such as the iconic image of Byron's brooding Romantic hero, Manfred, painted as *The Wanderer above a Sea of Mist* by Caspar David Friedrich (1818, Kunstshalle Hamburg). Lawrence painted the actor John Philip Kemble in Shakespearean roles, borrowing from the genre of history painting in so doing. History painting usually elevated scenes from the past, classical mythology and the Bible. Joseph Wright of Derby, instead, occasionally chose to paint subjects that showed the advances made in science, but one such painting, *An Experiment on a Bird in the Air-pump* (1768, National Gallery), has long been recognized as rather ambiguous in its praise of science. An itinerant lecturer is demonstrating to a well-to-do family how a vacuum can be created, using a bird in an air-pump. The lecturer is rather wild-looking; he stares out of the picture, looking directly at us in a rather challenging way, while his audience experience different reactions. The lecturer has removed air from the pump and the white cockatoo droops, suffering from the deprivation of oxygen. Among his audience, an older man sits looking down at the floor, leaning on his walking stick, thinking deeply and perhaps not positively about the march of science. Two girls turn away in horror from the scene while their father tries to persuade them to watch and learn.

Industrialization did not figure highly in the hierarchy of painting subjects, though Philip James de Loutherbourg's *Coalbrookdale by Night* (1801, Science Museum) shows the blast furnaces in Shropshire, representing them as a kind of hell. Loutherboug's paintings utilized Edmund Burke's aesthetic theory of the **sublime**, as set out in *A Philosophical Inquiry into the Origins of Our Ideas of the Sublime and the Beautiful* (1757), an extremely important text for Romantic painters and writers. Here, Burke argued that feelings of terror and dread evoke a powerful psychological response. Subjects such as seemingly infinite space, huge, overwhelming mountains, and wide, open seas, could elicit such a response. Protected from real danger by being at a safe distance, the viewer experiences a kind of mental blockage at the immensity of, say, the mountain or ocean, and the experience momentarily obliterates the viewer's sense of their self:

> The passion caused by the great and sublime in *nature*, when those causes operate most powerfully, is Astonishment; and astonishment is that state of the soul, in which all its motions are suspended, with some degree of horror. In this case the mind is so entirely filled with its object, that it cannot entertain any other, nor by consequence reason on that object which employs it. Hence arises the great power of the sublime, that, far from being produced by them, it anticipates our reasonings, and hurries us on by an irresistible force. (Burke 1999: 64)

Far from being a horrible experience, the dread that is felt gives way to 'delight' and the viewer is left changed by this encounter with the sublime. Burke's theories clearly owed much to his conservative notions of gender in which the **'beautiful'** is described as small, delicate and weak, while the sublime is a masculine 'Power' and is characterized as dominant, controlling and strong.

Constable and Turner

Two painters from the Romantic era, Joseph Mallord William Turner and John Constable, are among the most famous of all British painters and have become national institutions since their deaths – Turner has his own permanent exhibition housed in London's Tate Britain (the Clore Gallery), while Constable's pictures of rural Suffolk are commonly reproduced on placemats and greeting cards. The latter's reputation and popularity is now more secure than it was in his day and his paintings have come to symbolize an idealized image of Britain. His landscapes often show people working on the land, as in *Boat Building on the Stour* (1814, Victoria and Albert Museum), or evidence of human life in a natural scene, as in *Flatford Mill from a Lock on the Stour* (*circa* 1811, Victoria and Albert Museum). He attempted to capture the immediacy of a moment or experience, and was intensely aware of nature's endless variety, of its constantly changing light and mood. In this attempt to fix or make permanent a specific time or place, his art has been likened to the poetry of Wordsworth. In one of the most famous of his large paintings (commonly called the 'six-footers'), his *Hay Wain* 1821, (National Gallery), nature is as important, if not more important, than the solitary human figure on the hay cart. Constable endeavoured to represent nature faithfully and accurately, often sketching in oils in the open air so as to ensure that his representations of the skies were as naturalistic as possible.

Constable's naturalism can be contrasted with Turner's increasingly non-naturalistic style. Turner had great range, painting subjects that were both urban and rural, from history, classical literature, or scripture, and perhaps most famously his swirling seascapes. He was prolific (he has left nearly 300 sketchbooks filled with sketches often made in watercolour on the spot) and was the most famous painter of his day. His paintings were 'Romantic' in a different sense from Constable's. There are many paintings of places abroad, including images of Italy that speak of the Romantics' fascination with crumbling ruins, depictions of lost civilizations and ancient empires. *Decline of the Carthaginian Empire* (1815, National Gallery) is one such painting, which has been interpreted as a comment upon the fall of Napoleon's empire. Turner's sea-crossings to France inspired many of his dramatic seascapes, featuring stormy skies that are often indiscernible from tempestuous seas. These everyday scenes become portentous and full of significance. Blending the genres of history and landscape, paintings like *Snow Storm: Hannibal and his Army Crossing the Alps* (1812, Tate Gallery) show tiny human figures almost engulfed by the most extreme weather conditions. Turner's politics can be seen in such paintings as *Slavers Throwing Overboard the Dead and Dying – Typhon Coming On*, also known as 'The Slave Ship' (1839, Museum of Fine Arts, Boston), which registers his abhorrence of the slave trade, and in paintings that take their subject from ancient Greece, suggesting his sympathy with the Greek fight for national independence from the Ottoman Empire in the 1820s.

Both Turner and Constable included in their paintings elements of what was known as the '**picturesque**'. William Gilpin, in his *Observations on the River Wye* (1782), argued that nature could be improved upon, and encouraged painters to feature ruggedness, irregularity and variation in their paintings. Uvedale Price, writing his *Essay on the Picturesque* (1794), rather insensitively considered wandering 'beggars, gypsies, and all such rough tattered figures' as picturesque 'objects'; their inclusion in a landscape would offer the required detail for a picturesque work (Price 1794: 70). Such comments make clear how the rural poor and those who worked on the land were considered by those intent on creating an idealized or aesthetically pleasing version of Britain's countryside. Such theories were also influential in the gardening of Humphrey Repton who succeeded Lancelot 'Capability' Brown as the foremost landscape designer of the period, and whose landscapes were designed to look as though they were part of a picture.

Engraving

There were many challenges to the pre-eminence of the Royal Academy. William Blake was one artist who refused to accept its authority, particularly when it denied admittance to engravers, thus relegating them to the category of artisans rather than the creators of 'high art'. In response, the short-lived Society for Engravers was established in 1803. Blake believed in engraving as an art in its own right, rather than thinking of it as simply the mechanical reproduction of pictures. His own practice was innovative and independent, using old-fashioned techniques of line-engraving as well as new relief etching techniques. He illustrated his poems, such as *Songs of Innocence and of Experience* (1789–94), with images that bear a complicated and interpretative relationship to the poetry they accompany. Many of Blake's images were drawn from Milton and the Bible, and were visionary, prophetic and spiritual rather than naturalistic. Alternatively, the engraver Thomas Bewick used wood-block engraving to illustrate books of natural history with more attention to detail and accuracy, including *A General History of Quadrupeds* (1790) and *History of British Birds* (two volumes, 1797 and 1804). Reviewing the former in an *Analytical Review* of 1790, Mary Wollstonecraft mentioned specifically the 'number of beautiful wood cuts, executed with a degree of taste and simplicity, superior to any thing of the kind we have before seen in this country' (Wollstonecraft 1989, vol. 7: 260). Indeed, scientific and medical books often contained many illustrations that were important to the student's or practitioner's understanding of their subject. Books of poetry and prose were also often illustrated by artists, who were encouraged by new printing techniques. Paintings, too, could be reproduced in smaller, engraved versions, and this wider dissemination of art, coupled with the founding of the National Gallery in 1824, meant that more people from a broader spectrum of British society could view the art that was produced.

Political cartoons

Political cartoons were another art form that could be viewed easily by the general public, at least in London. Caricatures of the British monarchy, the aristocracy, politicians, lawyers and physicians were hung in the windows of print shops where all could see them – and they were also bought as luxury items by the very class that they satirized. The cartoons of George Cruikshank, James Gillray and Thomas Rowlandson were important predecessors of the political cartoons that now accompany our newspaper articles. Gillray, in particular, fostered a sense of national identity in his portrayal of John Bull as a helpless and patriotic farmer, the casualty of his government's tax policies and national debt. His identity as a symbol of Britain is further determined by his opposite: the skinny, garlic-eating, smooth-talking, tricolour-wearing, sexually rapacious Frenchman, and such cartoons were used as propaganda in the war with France during this period. Napoleon was often figured as a diminutive madman, in one cartoon carving up the world between himself and the British prime minister, William Pitt the Younger (*The Plumb-Pudding in Danger*, 1805, Library of Congress).

Music and the theatre

Most of the classical composers who wrote music that spoke to the concerns of this period lived in continental Europe, such as Ludwig van Beethoven, Joseph Hadyn, Wolfgang Amadeus Mozart and Felix Mendelssohn. The music written by these European men tended to be heard in England in select gatherings, such as at the aristocratic country house or the exclusive Concert of Ancient Music, which gave concerts to London's high society. There was, though, a move to more public musical events, with tickets priced at different levels allowing for a greater number of merchants and others to attend.

One form of entertainment that was open to a more popular audience was the theatre. Indeed, the theatre had rather a bad reputation in London as a venue for prostitution and gambling. Government and religious ministers denounced it not only because of these social ills but also because the plays produced often reflected or criticized the political events of the times. Even some plays by Shakespeare were considered too inflammatory to be performed. The social hierarchy was rigidly adhered to with the differently priced tickets for the private boxes of the wealthy, the pit for the merchant or professional classes, and the gallery for everyone else – when Covent Garden attempted to raise the price of tickets in 1809, a riot broke out. There were a number of successful dramatists, including Joanna Baillie, George Colman the Younger, Thomas Holcroft, Elizabeth Inchbald, Douglas Jerrold, Sheridan Knowles and Richard Brinsley Sheridan; although, traditionally, Romantic drama has not been given as much critical attention as other genres, this is one area that has recently seen far greater interest.

Newspapers and novels

New technologies in printing and a wider literacy among the population encouraged the growth of a number of new newspapers and journals, promoting an interest in politics at home and abroad, and in science and culture in general. The increased number of authors and readers alarmed governments at the time; the Society for the Suppression of Vice was set up privately to discover instances of supposed blasphemy, sedition and immorality. Radical writers such as William Cobbett, Richard Carlile, William Hone and Francis Place lived in constant fear of being arrested, and during their lives spent time in prison. This period also saw the writing and reading of novels rise, though they were held by some to be vulgar and sensational. Circulating libraries meant that many people could borrow fiction and non-fiction books which they could not otherwise afford to buy. (Novels are dealt with in more detail in Chapter 2).

Travel: trade and exploration

While much exploration in the Romantic period was under-taken primarily for trade purposes, travel literature and accounts of cultures abroad had a discernible effect on British culture. Tea, sugar, spices and silks were also brought back and consumed. The vogue for all things exotic revealed itself in the fashion for Malaysian tables in the houses of the English aristocracy and in the country's architecture. Public 'pleasure gardens', such as those at Vauxhall in London, where people were charged entry to an area of walks, music, shows and other entertainments, reflected this interest by adopting a Tahitian theme. John Nash remodelled the Royal Pavilion in Brighton in oriental style for the Prince of Wales. Captain James Cook had undertaken three important jour-neys to the Pacific in 1768–71, 1772–5 and 1776–80, which significantly increased knowledge of the customs and soci-eties of indigenous peoples, of the natural flora and fauna of these lands, and of astronomy. Accompanying Cook on his first expedition to the South Seas, the botanist Joseph Banks increased by nearly 25 per cent the number of known plant species (Fulford, Lee and Kitson 2004: 36). These were truly exciting times and the aims of Cook's expeditions were grand and extensive. He hoped to observe the transit of Venus, cir-cumnavigate the globe from west to east, find the north-west passage by sea from the Pacific to the Atlantic Ocean, and disprove the existence of a great southern continent.

The stories of encounters with the peoples of other conti-nents were greedily consumed by British readers. Mungo Parks' stories of his travels to discover new possibilities for British trade in the interior of Africa were sentimental nar-ratives in which his faith in God came to his aid when faced with alien and dangerous natives. Travel narratives were often salacious, filled with accounts of the depravity of native peoples, described as being in a more primitive or barbaric stage of civilization than the white Europeans. Even when represented as a kind of 'noble savage', a concept that was put forward by Jean-Jacque Rousseau, the stereotypes of native peoples was racist and condescending. One of the most enduring travel stories is that of the Mutiny on the *Bounty*, a ship commanded by Captain William Bligh, which journeyed to Tahiti in order to bring breadfruit from Tahiti to the West Indies to feed slaves there more cheaply. Bligh's now legendary tyranny in the command of the ship, coupled with the men's enjoyment of the sensual pleasures offered by the island, has been exaggerated, but Bligh's extraordinary escape in the small, open boat in which he was set adrift still captures the imagination. Tahiti was represented in contemporary literature as an Edenic paradise where the land was so fertile that no one needed to work, and the women were sexually freer; the first Christian missionaries in Tahiti failed because the Englishmen kept running off with native women (quite literally kidnapping them in many cases), before Banks authorized the sending over of British women as wives to solve the problem (Fulford, Lee and Kitson 2004: 120). The result of the British 'discovery' of Tahiti was to introduce sexually transmitted diseases, prostitution and the loss of the people's knowledge of traditional methods of building. This story was repeated elsewhere.

Britain had more established links with India because the East India Company, set up in 1600, had by the end of the seventeenth century secured trade through military force, and at the start of the Romantic period controlled huge parts of India. The British in India had acquired a poor reputation, particularly after the very public trial of Warren Hastings, the Governor of Bengal. Evidence given in the smear campaign against him represented the British officials in India as corrupt and promiscuous. The armchair travellers of the Romantic period were fascinated with scurrilous and sensational tales of the 'East'; a term that could be used to refer to Turkish, Persian, Indian, Chinese and Japanese cultures. As this suggests, the 'East' or the 'Orient' (see **orientalism**) was a rather oversimplified term, constructed by its opposition to an equally oversimplified idea of the 'West', as Edward Said has argued in *Orientalism* (1978). Accounts of the East in the period's literature construct an alien 'Other' in opposition to a western 'Self'. In fact, representations of the 'East', its places, peoples and cultures, actually tell us more about the identities of Western creators and consumers. It is figured as tyrannical, sensual, exotic, inexplicable and barbaric in such hugely popular poems as Byron's *Corsair* (1814) or Thomas Moore's *Lalla Rookh* (1817). In contrast, William Jones spent his life learning the languages of India, where he worked as a judge in the Bengal Supreme Court, translating Indian poetry and compiling a digest of the local laws, by which he thought native peoples should be more fairly tried. Jones founded the Asiatic Society of Bengal in 1784, and his emphasis was always on the originality of the sources that he translated. He succeeded in demonstrating that Sanskrit shared a common origin with the languages on which Western languages were based, Greek and Latin, thus displacing the notion of Western culture as the original and founding one. His efforts were part of 'oriental renaissance' during this period, which is also revealed in novels such as William Beckford's *Vathek* (1781) and Elizabeth Hamilton's *Letters of a Hindoo Rajah* (1797), containing extensive learned notes explaining Hindu customs, and in the enthusiasm for Indian music that took over the parties of British families in Calcutta in the 1780s. Orientalism in the period, though, is generally characterized by an attempt to impose British values on a society represented as inferior, reinforcing stereotypes and models of imperialist power.

Britain's fascination with travel and exploration in the Romantic era had an influence on many different aspects of its culture. Josiah Wedgwood's pottery, for example, was modelled on ancient Greek, Etruscan and Roman pottery that had been unearthed in archaeological digs. He copied urns that had been brought back to Britain by travellers. This period saw an interest in **neo-classicism** or **Hellenism** that revived the designs, literature and arts of ancient civilizations, in the belief that the Greek age was a 'golden age' of artistic achievement. Ancient Greece was seen as a time of unparalleled freedom and liberty, its republic admired by writers such as Byron and Percy Shelley. In 1816, Lord Elgin sold the so-called 'Elgin Marbles', which he had acquired in rather dubious fashion from the Parthenon at Athens, for the British Government, and they are still housed, controversially, in the British Museum in London. The sight of these sculptures had a considerable effect on John Keats, who wrote about them in 'On First Seeing the Elgin Marbles' (1817). In architecture, the classical style produced buildings with mock-temple fronts supported by pillars, such as William Wilkins' creations University College London (1827–8) and the National Gallery (1834–8), George Saunders' Townley Gallery for the British Museum (1804–8) and John Soane's Bank of England (1788–1833).

Excavations had revealed the ash-covered victims of the volcanic explosion at Pompeii, and many Romantic writers journeyed to Naples and the south of Italy to see these sights and the spectacular Mount Vesuvius. Felicia Hemans was one Romantic poet who was inspired by the accounts of Pompeii, such as in her poem 'The Image in Lava' (1827), for example. There was also an interest in the past of Britain, which helped in the formation of national identities for Scotland, Wales, England and Ireland. There was a search to find antiquities which could prove that Britain, too, had been an ancient civilization. James McPherson translated and published a collection of poems in the 1750s and 1760s that he claimed had been written by the third-century Gaelic poet Ossian; it later emerged that these were forgeries. Attempting to find an English equivalent, Thomas Percy published a collection of ballads under the title *Reliques of Ancient English Poetry* (1765), claiming that these were the work of ancient English bards; he, too, came under criticism for altering the authentic manuscripts when he published them. Novels such as Sydney Owenson's *The Wild Irish Girl: A National Tale* (1806), with its extensive footnotes giving information on Irish history, mythology and language, helped foster a national pride in Irish culture.

The revival of **Gothic** styles was part of the Romantic interest in the medieval and can be seen as part of the emerging national identity Britain was forging during the time it was at war with France. Gothic principles were picturesque, emphasizing variation, roughness or ruggedness, rather than polished finish, and asymmetry. One eclectic example is Strawberry Hill, the home of Horace Walpole who wrote the first Gothic novel, *The Castle of Otranto* (1764). Walpole extended and rebuilt parts of this house in Twickenham until it became a small Gothic castle, with battlements and towers.

2

Literature in the Romantic Period

Major Genres
Movements and Literary Groups

MAJOR GENRES

This section begins by considering the formation of a new hybrid poetic genre, the *Lyrical Ballad*. Attention is also given to other forms of poetry that emerged or were revived in the period, such as the sonnets of Charlotte Smith, the conversation poems of S. T. Coleridge, the ode, satire, and Blake's *Songs*. The section also investigates the claims made for poetry, looking at the emergence of the novel form, with particular reference to the Gothic novel, psychological thrillers, Jane Austen's novel of manners, and Walter Scott's historical novels, as well as the importance of political prose writing during the period. Finally, this section recognizes the popularity of drama in the period, examining the kinds of plays performed, and ends with a brief look at 'drama of the mind', such as Byron's *Manfred*.

Poetry: Ballads

Poetry has traditionally been regarded as the most 'Romantic' of the genres in which people wrote, but this is due more to the preferences of later critics than the reading public of the time. Some of the poems that are now most celebrated, such as those written by the canonical male poets Blake, Wordsworth, Coleridge, Byron, Shelley and Keats, were not especially widely known during the period. Indeed, some of the now most famous, such as Wordsworth's *Prelude* or Shelley's *Mask of Anarchy*, were not published until many years after they had first been composed and when their authors were dead. Even at the time, poets did regard themselves as distinct from other writers; Shelley wrote in *A Defence of Poetry* that he regarded poets as the 'unacknowledged legislators of the World' (Norton 2006, vol. 2: 850), and Wordsworth, in the 1802 Preface to the *Lyrical Ballads*, describes a poet as 'a man [. . .] endued with more lively sensibility, more enthusiasm and tenderness, who has a greater knowledge of human nature, and a more comprehensive soul, than are supposed to be common among mankind' (Norton 2006, vol. 2: 269). One of the most universally acclaimed abilities of poets during this period was their ability to feel for others, to imagine themselves in others' situations and predicaments.

In the 'Advertisement' to the first edition of the *Lyrical Ballads*, Wordsworth warned readers that they might 'frequently have to struggle with feelings of strangeness and awkwardness', indicating that the poetry he and Coleridge were publishing in this collection was different to anything their audience would have encountered before (Wu 2006: 331). Indeed, Wordsworth wrote that the poems should be 'considered as experiments' (Wu 2006: 331). When this 'Advertisement' was extended to a Preface, the poet developed his ideas further and argued that this collection of poems should be thought of as diverging deliberately and radically from the **neo-classical** traditions of the eighteenth century. Wordsworth was experimenting in a number of ways; he had determined to write in 'the real language of men', in the language 'really used by men', and 'as a man speaking to men' (Norton 2006, vol. 2: 263, 264, 269). He was not alone in arguing that a new style of poetic language and poetic genre was required; there is evidence that many writers were engaged in such debates. Joanna Baillie, Anna

Seward and Joseph Weston were among those who published new theories of poetry. These theories can be seen as more progressive than Wordsworth's because they also recognize the importance of women's literary and dramatic writing. In general, the Romantics reacted against the neo-classical traditions of such writers as Alexander Pope and John Dryden. The eighteenth century had revived classical genres such as the satire and the **ode**, and writers had produced highly structured poems that appealed to the intellect. These were written in an elevated language, often in heroic couplets (rhyming lines of iambic pentameter), and often with an educative or moral purpose (see Pope's *Essay on Man* for a good example of this kind of poem). Of course, not all Romantic writers shunned their literary predecessors; Byron, for one, was highly influenced by eighteenth-century satire but, in general, the Romantic period can be seen as a return to feeling, and a new, intense subjective response to the natural world.

Wordsworth and Coleridge, in describing their poems as 'Lyrical Ballads', were creating a new, hybrid genre. They were breaking away from the traditions of previous centuries in which writers had seen genres as fixed forms that had rules and conventions; and the closest that a writer came to imitating the strict form of the genre, the more successful his or her achievement. The **ballad** had particular associations for poets. Traditionally, ballads were folk-songs, many of which had been handed down through time orally rather than being written down. They were often in simple language, anonymous, told from an impersonal narrative perspective, sometimes describing a single event, and used repeated phrases and a regular pattern of metre and rhythm (often alternate lines of tetrameter and trimeter with the second and fourth line rhyming), all of which ensured that these poems could be easily remembered. During this period, Scottish and English ballads were collected and published by such figures as Thomas Percy and Walter Scott in an effort to revive a national heritage. As all this suggests, the ballad was not a form that any self-respecting eighteenth-century poet would have used; it was not a classical form revived from the Ancient Greek or Roman poets, but a folk tradition associated not with the elite classes but the lower orders.

In choosing this mode, Wordsworth and Coleridge were making a political gesture, and the subjects of the *Lyrical Ballads* (a mad mother, idiot boy, convict and female vagrant, among others) were not those usually written about in poetry. In *The Spirit of the Age* (1825), William Hazlitt described Wordsworth's muse as 'a levelling one', which 'proceeds on a principle of equality'; as such, 'It partakes of, and is carried along with, the revolutionary movement of our age' (Hazlitt 1991: 139). The Preface to the *Lyrical Ballads* spoke of poetry as a 'spontaneous overflow of powerful feelings' in contrast to the explicit artifice and wit of the poetry of Wordsworth's predecessors, and the poems were largely concerned with the rural poor, the neglected labourers and unemployed of the countryside rather than the aristocracy or inhabitants of the cities (Norton 2006, vol. 2: 265). In 'Michael: A Pastoral Poem', one of the poems added to the second edition of the *Lyrical Ballads* in 1800, Michael's son is lost to his father when he leaves the Lake District for London: 'in the dissolute city gave himself / To evil courses' (Norton 2006, vol. 2: 301). Traditional ballads were woven into new verse; for example, the famous ballad of 'Sir Patrick Spence' is quoted at the beginning of Coleridge's 'Dejection: An Ode'.

The lyric and the sonnet

The other part of this new hybrid genre should not be neglected; these ballads were also 'lyrical'. A lyric poem is a seemingly private, honest and true emotional response, spoken from the heart by a first-person narrator. Wordsworth's 'Resolution and Independence' is a good example of this; a poem which openly declares the poet's despondent feelings about himself, his life and his role as a poet. J. S. Mill described a lyric poem as one in which the poet seems to be 'overheard' by an audience; in other words, the poet offers the true state of their mind without knowingly presenting it in a particular way.

> The peculiarity of poetry appears to us to lie in the poet's utter unconsciousness of a listener. Poetry is feeling confessing itself to itself in moments of solitude, and embodying itself in symbols which are the nearest possible representations of the feeling in the exact shape in which it exists in the poet's mind. (Norton 2006, vol. 2: 1048)

An example of such poetry is that written by Charlotte Smith (1749–1806), although her poems also belong to the literary movement of **Sensibility**, an eighteenth-century movement that continued into the Romantic period and which privileged feeling over reason. Smith's *Elegiac Sonnets* were published in 1784 at her own expense in an attempt to raise money. Her publishing efforts were to sustain her family's social standing while awaiting the outcome (which did not come within her lifetime) of a chancery court case that would restore her to the status and wealth of a gentlewoman. Her husband was profligate with money and Smith had spent part of the previous year in a debtor's prison with him (Zimmerman 2004).

In the *Elegiac Sonnets*, Smith presented herself autobiographically as a solitary, world-weary, mournful and melancholy poet-figure. In the sonnet 'On Being Cautioned against Walking on an Headland Overlooking the Sea, Because it was Frequented by a Lunatic', for example, the narrator imagines the plight of this poor, 'solitary wretch', the 'Lunatic':

Is there a solitary wretch who hies
    To the tall cliff, with starting pace or slow,
And, measuring, views with wild and hollow eyes
    Its distance from the waves that chide below;
Who, as the sea-born gale with frequent sighs
    Chills his cold bed upon the mountain turf,
With hoarse, half-utter'd lamentation, lies

Murmuring responses to the dashing surf?
In moody sadness, on the giddy brink,
I see him more with envy than with fear;
He has no *nice felicities* that shrink
From giant horrors; wildly wandering here,
He seems (uncursed with reason) not to know
The depth or the duration of his woe.
(Norton 2006, vol. 2: 41–2)

Smith imagines the madman 'measuring' the distance between the cliff and sea below, suggesting perhaps that he is considering jumping off and ending it all. She not only sympathizes with him but indeed envies him; his lack of reason means that he is not aware of 'The depth or the duration of his woe'. There is a paradox here: can he both be so unhappy that he wishes to commit suicide and unaware of how awful his life is? We realize through the fact that she does not at any point see the actual 'Lunatic', that she is actually describing her own feelings as though they were his. Her apparent sympathy with his state of mind is actually a projection of her own unhappiness onto this perhaps fictional character she has been warned about. The question with which she begins her poem, 'Is there a solitary wretch who hies [. . .]' is answered with a yes, but she herself is the wretch in question, wandering upon a headland rebelliously although she has been cautioned against it.

Her particular situation as a woman is also alluded to here, in the fact that she has been warned not to walk in particular areas and in the imagery she uses: the wives 'chide' or tell her off, while she laments her femininity. She wishes she did not have the '*nice felicities* that shrink / From giant horrors'. Perhaps they are all that stop her from being brave enough to throw herself off the 'giddy brink' on which she stands. Here we can see how Smith creates a persona which seems to have much to do with her own life of pain and suffering. In lyric poetry such as this, the poet is constantly betraying themselves to their audience, their personal feelings and emotions coming through even in the descriptions of a

natural landscape or character. In 'On Being Cautioned
[. . .]', for example, the 'sea-born gale' frequently 'sighs',
reflecting the mood of the poet. Smith's use of and experi-
mentation with the sonnet form did much to bring it back
into fashion. *Elegiac Sonnets* ran into nine editions and greatly
influenced the sonnets of Wordsworth, Coleridge and Keats.

The subjectivity of these lyric poems is something that dis-
tinguishes them from dramatic poems. Robert Browning, in
his 'Essay on Shelley', made a distinction between a 'subjective' poet and an 'objective' poet; the first is like a prophet or
seer, 'impelled to embody that which he perceives', and this
kind of poetry 'cannot be easily considered in abstraction'
from the poet's personality, such as we have seen with Smith's
poem (Browning 1981, vol. 5: 137, 138, 139). An 'objective'
poet, on the other hand, is a kind of fashioner who creates a
character and makes them speak; there is nothing of the poet
in the character. In an 1818 letter to Richard Woodhouse,
Keats also identified two kinds of poets: one of which he
describes as the Wordsworthian or 'egotistical sublime'
(Norton 2006, vol. 2: 947). Keats does not place himself
within this category of poet. An 'egotist' is defined in the
Oxford English Dictionary as 'one who thinks or talks too much
of himself'. In another letter to John Hamilton Reynolds
(dated 3 February) that speaks of Wordsworth as an 'egotist',
Keats writes:

> Poetry should be great and unobtrusive, a thing which enters
> into one's soul, and does not startle it or amaze it with itself but
> with its subject. How beautiful are the retired flowers! How
> would they lose their beauty were they to throng into the
> highway crying out, 'Admire me, I am a violet!', 'Dote upon me,
> I am a primrose!' (Norton 2006, vol. 2: 943)

For Keats, a poet of the 'egotistical sublime' is 'a thing per se'
which 'stands alone': it is a thing in itself, without need of any
other agency to create or sustain it (Norton 2006, vol. 2: 947).
Coleridge and Wordsworth are examples of subjective poets
where the ego governs and unifies poetic experience. Nature

and the external world are experienced through the poet. The other kind of poetical character is the category to which Keats believes he (and Shakespeare) belong, one that he calls the 'camelion poet' (Norton 2006, vol. 2: 947). This character has no self, is not a whole individual who can stand alone but instead belongs nowhere, inhabits many different skins and has no identity of its own. Just as chameleons can change the colour of their skin to adapt to their environments, these poets can assume the identity of the character they write about. They are less concerned with talking of themselves and more concerned with the feelings and lives of others. This distinction can be seen as a fundamental division between poets. John Clare is another who might be regarded as a 'camelion poet'; instead of making himself the subject of the poem and being concerned with nature only in so far as it reflects this self, Clare often writes as if he were nature, speaking from the perspective of the land and the animals that live on it, enjoying nature for its own sake.

Conversation poems

Many Romantic forms of poetry were deliberately not elevated in their language and style, such as the 'conversation poems' of Coleridge, a form that can be linked to the sparse and colloquial style of the ballad. Coleridge's poems 'The Nightingale: A Conversational Poem'; 'This Lime-Tree Bower, My Prison'; 'Frost at Midnight' and 'The Eolian Harp' are among those included in this sub-genre of poetry. These poems tend to be very specific about the place and time in which they are composed, usually the poet is outdoors, often with friends, and they are written in blank verse paragraphs of different lengths (unrhymed lines of iambic pentameter). They continued the project undertaken by Wordsworth and Coleridge to write as men really spoke, in a conversational style, as though speaking to a friend. We seem to hear Coleridge speaking to Dorothy and William Wordsworth in an unplanned and spontaneous fashion, hearing his apparently artless and sincere words. These poems should remind us that the solitary lyric poet was not the only figure to be heard; the Romantics also attempted by their writings to create communities of like-minded individuals.

The ode

The 'ode' was a classical form made popular by the ancient poets Pindar and Horace, but the Romantics changed and adapted it for their own uses. Pindar's odes were elevated in their style and subject matter, with a rigorous structure made up of three movements sung by a Chorus, while Horatian odes were more muted in style, more conversational in their choice of words and more contemplative in their manner. A good example of the Pindaric ode with its *strophe* ('turn'), *antistrophe* ('counter-turn') and *epode* ('stand') is Ben Jonson's 'To the Immortal Memory and Friendship of that Noble Pair, Sir Lucius Cary and Sir H. Morison' (Norton 2006, vol. 1: 1439–43). The seventeenth-century poet Abraham Cowley's later version of the Pindaric and Horatian odes created the more irregular verse form that the Romantics preferred.

An ode is usually addressed to something specific but the poet uses this occasion to express his or her feelings, thoughts and mood. The odes of Mary Robinson (1756/1758?–1800), for example, are addressed to 'the Muse', 'Melancholy', and 'the Nightingale', Keats's to a 'Grecian Urn' or 'Nightingale', and Shelley's to a 'Sky Lark' or 'West Wind'. Romantic odes are often self-reflexive, musing on poetry though explicitly contemplating a work of art, such as the urn, or the song of a bird. In 'Ode on a Grecian Urn', Keats attempts to read the urn as a text, asking questions of all art as he does so. He struggles to work out what the urn is telling him, what is its message, or the moral of its tale. He questions whether art can transcend time and be relevant beyond its original moment of reception. Is the urn symbolic of art; can it fix a perfect moment in time and make it last for ever? Clearly, these questions are relevant to all art, including Keats's poem itself. In Shelley's ode, 'To a

Skylark', the poet wishes that he could sing as the bird does, but recognizes that, like Keats's nightingale, the only reason that birds sing in this way is because they have not experienced the pain and suffering that humans experience. Robinson's nightingale, in contrast, is a 'Sweet Bird of Sorrow!', whose song finds a sympathetic response in the sad song of Robinson's ode (Robinson 2000: 82). In these writers' hands the ode evolved into a characteristically Romantic poetic form, not simply because of their innovations in style, such as Keats's ten-line stanza in 'Ode on a Grecian Urn', but also because of the way that contemplation of a single object led the poet outwards and beyond into meditations upon life and art.

Satire

One classical genre which displayed a public and social voice of the poet was satire, most associated with the Roman poets Juvenal and Horace. Peter Pindar, the pseudonym under which the poet John Wolcot wrote, was one of the period's most famous political satirists. Political events provided much material for satire, whether in the cartoons of Gillray and Cruikshank or the verses printed in journals. Many of Byron's satirical writings, such as the 'Dedication' and Canto One of *Don Juan*, focus on the reviewers of his poetry and the poets he saw as reactionary and staid, such as Southey and Wordsworth. *Don Juan* used the *ottava rima* verse form, eight-line stanzas where the first six lines rhyme alternately but the final two lines are a rhyming couplet. This allows for a swift reversal of the first part of the stanza, and is often where the comedy is to be found. Other forms were more gentle in their humour, such as the mock-epic poem 'Washing Day' by Anna Barbauld, in which the women's elevation of washing into a subject fit for the muses (who have 'turned gossips') to sing of is ridiculed, but this is tempered by the personal recollections of her childhood and the insight given into the private, domestic world of women (Norton 2006, vol. 2: 37).

Songs

Blake's *Songs of Innocence and of Experience* (1789–94) highlighted the social problems that he saw in London, such as
the hazardous employment of children as chimney sweeps,
in a form that might not seem to be obviously critical of such
a practice. These poems appear to be for children; 'The
Chimney Sweeper' of the *Songs of Innocence* is written from the
perspective of an older chimney sweep, comforting 'little
Tom Dacre' who has just arrived and is new to the work
(Norton 2006, vol. 2: 85). Tom dreams that night of escape
from the chimneys, symbolized by 'coffins of black', and of
an angel who delivers him a message which makes him
'happy & warm' (Norton 2006, vol. 2: 85). The message is
that 'if he'd be good boy, / He'd have God for his father &
never want joy' (Norton 2006, vol. 2: 85). Though it is never
said in the poem, the implication is that this message, while
comforting, offers an empty promise; indeed, it is little more
than a veiled threat, telling Tom that if he does not behave,
he will be sorry. The moralizing poems and stories written for
children in these times often offered such instruction, and
here Blake offers up to us the effects of the 'mind-forged
manacles' which such innocents as Tom and the narrator
display ('London', Norton 2006, vol. 2: 94). Blake's *Songs*
seem as though they were written for children, often using a
long hymnal measure (alternate rhyming lines of iambic
tetrameter); but their simplicity belies the strength and vigour
of their criticism of Church and state.

These poems were accompanied by Blake's engravings,
which add to and complicate our interpretation of the *Songs*.
For example, the plate that accompanies 'The Ecchoing
Green' in *Songs of Innocence*, is framed by a large tree, very full
and thick with leaves in the height of summer. It is a particularly healthy-looking tree, which fills the picture from left to
right canopying the children playing beneath it, while the
adults sit beneath it on seats which seem to be made out of
its trunk. The tree extends beyond the limits of the plate's
frame; you cannot see it in its entirety, because the furthest

reaches of its top left and right branches are outside the picture. This tree is protective, offering shelter to those beneath it, but it also completely encloses them from the outside world, and does not allow any external influence to affect the community under its protection. Edward Larrisy has argued that these closeting frames imply that a constrictive force governs the state of innocence being described within the poem (Larrisy 1985). Verses published in giftbooks such as *The Keepsake* annuals of poetry were also accompanied by illustrations. Some of the most celebrated poets of the day were published in these, including Letitia Elizabeth Landon ('L.E.L') (1802–38) and Felicia Hemans. The books were lavish productions, made specifically for middle-class women as gifts.

Prose: the novel

The novel was one of the most popular genres in this period and was particularly popular with women, as can be seen from the many parodies of female readers in novels of the time. When we are told that the protagonist's imagination has been overstimulated by reading novels, as is the case with Catherine Moreland in Jane Austen's *Northanger Abbey* (1818), it is clear that there were many who believed with Wordsworth that novels were 'frantic', their readers characterized by a 'degrading thirst after outrageous stimulation' (Norton 2006, vol. 2: 266). As Wordsworth's comment suggests, novels were held in little regard by some, though the historical novels of Walter Scott helped to improve their image. Despite this, they were read widely; readers could obtain them from circulating libraries rather than having to purchase them, and the popularity of the novel was aided in this period by the increase in literacy and the improvements in publishing technology. There is evidence to suggest that three times as many new novels were published in 1790 as in 1750 (Jarvis 2004: 50–1). Literacy levels improved to such an extent that by 1830 the national average for male literacy was around 65 per cent and female literacy was around 50 per cent (Jarvis 2004: 58). Robin Jarvis speculates that the specific interest in novels was due to 'the understandable lure of fantasy and romance, the otherworldliness of narrative' that appealed to 'the growing numbers of urbanized workers living in squalid conditions' (Jarvis 2004: 59). The change in copyright law in 1774 meant that the work of dead writers could be published by anyone and there were increased numbers of multi-volumed series which republished such writers as Henry Fielding and Samuel Richardson.

Gothic novels

Caleb in William Godwin's *Caleb Williams*, rather like Catherine Moreland, is another character who has learned what he knows of life from novels, and this information reveals him to be rather naïve, trusting and even a little effeminate. In many ways, Caleb occupies the role of the female victim in a Gothic novel, a form that came into its own during the period. Horace Walpole's *Castle of Otranto* (1765) is generally agreed to be the first in this genre, and others continued and developed it, such as Charlotte Dacre (1782?–1825), Matthew 'Monk' Lewis (1775–1818) and Ann Radcliffe (1764–1823). John Aikin and Anna Barbauld wrote about the 'apparent delight with which we dwell upon objects of pure terror, where our moral feelings are not in the least concerned, and no passion seems to be excited but the depressing one of fear' (Aikin and Barbauld 1773). The pleasing terror occasioned by Gothic novels can be likened to the awe inspired by the **sublime** as described by Edmund Burke (see Chapter 1), which allowed one to enjoy being terrified.

The interest in the supernatural can be likened to other Romantic projects. Coleridge's 'The Rime of the Ancient Mariner', published in the *Lyrical Ballads*, was specifically interested in the supernatural. In *Biographia Literaria*, Coleridge recalled that the collection would include two types of poetry, one in which 'subjects were to be chosen from ordinary life', but for the other, the incidents and agents were to be (in part at least) supernatural – and the excellence aimed at was to consist in the interesting of the affections by the dramatic truth of such emotions as would naturally accompany such situations, supposing them real. (Wu 2006: 692)

This interest in observing the effects of an encountering with the supernatural continued in Radcliffe's novels, in which the supposed supernatural agency is, by the end of the novel, revealed to have a rational explanation. This technique has been called the 'explained supernatural'; it enabled her readers to enjoy the mystery and terror of the unknown while being returned safely to a world of Augustan reason and social norms by the end of the novel. In *The Italian* (1797), for example, in a rather conventional plot development, the novel's heroine, who has been kidnapped and almost killed because she is not of the right social class for marriage to the Countess's son, turns out to be descended from an ancient, noble family. In other aspects, Radcliffe's novels were more radical; her particular contribution to the Gothic novel genre is her formulation of what has been described as the 'female gothic' by Ellen Moers (Moers 1976). Locating the source of real terror in the novel within the domestic family unit seems peculiarly threatening to women rather than to men. Not only this, in *The Italian*, it is the heroine, Ellena, who demonstrates strength of mind and fortitude despite the misfortunes that befall her, while her lover Vivaldi is far more susceptible to the failings of sensibility and superstition that are usually associated with women.

The title page of the first edition of Walpole's novel claimed that this story was 'Translated by William Marshal, Gent. From the Original Italian of Onuphrio Muralto, Canon of the Church of St. Nicholas at Otranto', while the Preface claimed that the 'following work had been found in the library of an ancient catholic family in the North of England' and that it had been printed in 1529 (Walpole 1986: 37, 39). This pretence that the story was far older than it actually was, and that it was originally Italian, signified a world quite different from the one in which the novel was read. It deliberately harked back to dark times, times of ignorance and injustice, when people were superstitious and were ruled by the often sadistic and cruel secret trials and punishments of the Inquisition.

Psychological thrillers

There was a more general interest in the psychological aspects of character, with some innovations in narrative form. Even in Gothic novels where supernatural or seemingly supernatural events occurred, there was a real attempt to faithfully represent the mind's response to these unusual situations. *Caleb Williams*, again, reveals something of the mind of a beleaguered, paranoid man who is considered by all to be guilty of a crime he did not commit. Godwin's own life in these uneasy times, watching friends and fellow radicals being arrested, tried and, in some cases, transported for voicing their political opinion, can be found in the first-person narrative of Caleb. Mary Shelley used the same techniques in the framing narratives of *Frankenstein*; the authorial voice that might judge the events of the story is absent, and instead we have only the potentially unreliable narratives of monsters and madman enclosed within each other. The doubling of the Creature with Victor Frankenstein, where the two are locked into a relationship in which the pursuer becomes the pursued, is highly reminiscent of the relationship between Caleb and his vengeful master, Falkland. Other novels also played with narrative form to challenge the idea of the truthful narrator; *The Private Memoirs and Confessions of a Justified Sinner* (1824) by James Hogg (*bap.* 1770–1835) places the reader in the uncomfortable position of reading a first-hand account of a man who seems to be mentally unhinged.

The novel of manners

The novels of Jane Austen are still immensely popular with readers today, and many have been made into Hollywood blockbuster films. Austen's career moved from the early unpublished, epistolary novel more common in the eighteenth century ('Lady Susan'), through the light-hearted social comedy *Pride and Prejudice* (1813), to the somewhat darker moralizing of Fanny Price in *Mansfield Park* (1814). Austen's use of the witty and wise narrative voice pours scorn on upper-class society and even, at times, belittles her own heroines. Her innovative use of free indirect speech, where the feelings and perspective of the characters are subsumed within the third-person narrator's voice, often reveals the outsider's perspective on the upper classes. An often-referred-to military force, in the figures of army captains and navy admirals, intrudes upon a world of balls, spa towns and country houses in these novels, and demonstrates the author's interest in issues beyond the domestic and social. The novels often involve issues of inheritance and tradition, dramatizing the worries of Edmund Burke concerning Britain's move from the status quo while also revealing the inadequacy of many landlords and patriarchs. Although far from the forceful and direct politics of Wollstonecraft's *Vindication of the Rights of Woman*, Austen's ladies of leisure, such as Mrs Bennett in *Pride and Prejudice* and Lady Bertram in *Mansfield Park*, can be seen as novelized versions of the 'weak woman of fashion, who was more than commonly proud of her delicacy and sensibility' (Wollstonecraft 1997: 155).

The historical novels

Walter Scott has been seen as the creator of the historical novel. His first novel, *Waverly* (1814), was set in the past, and concerned the **Jacobite** rebellion in Scotland in 1745. While patriotically celebrating Scottish culture, its traditions and national identity, Scott's novel also faithfully represented his political perspective, which was sure of the benefits of the Anglo-Scottish Union. Scott had to imagine ways in which to represent a unified single British identity which allowed for, and yet incorporated, Scottish difference (see **Nationalism**). This political mission was one which he believed Maria

Edgeworth (1768–1849) had achieved for Ireland. It is as though the novel presents a historically and sociologically true and accurate picture of a race of people now gone from Britain, like the ancient Greeks or Romans. The character of Waverley is very clearly the new man – a symbol of modernity – and clearly he will survive where those who represent the ancient race, such as Fergus McIvor, will not. The tension Scott had to negotiate was between the ancient, feudal world of Scotland and the new, modern Scotland which was part of Britain.

Political writings

A great many political tracts were written during the early part of this period, before the 'Gagging Acts' were passed by the Government. Indeed, the period following Burke's *Reflections on the Revolution in France* (1790) was known for the 'pamphlet wars' that this text provoked. Many other texts had an overtly educational purpose, whether they were conduct books written for women or moral tales for children. Rousseau's influence can be seen in Maria Edgeworth's educational writings, *Practical Education*, written with her father in 1798, and *Moral Tales*, published for children in 1801. Hannah More published politically conservative texts such as her *Village Politics Addressed to All Mechanics, Journeymen, and Day Labourers* (1793) and *Cheap Repository Tracts* (1795–7), written to promote her reactionary support of Burke, her Evangelical religious beliefs, and her fight against feminism and republicanism. Such texts set out to reinforce traditional gender stereotypes and hierarchical class structures and were used as propaganda in the war against France. Another political writer who wrote for the audience to which More appealed in many of her texts – the mechanics, journeymen and labourers that *Village Politics* was addressed to – was William Cobbett. Cobbett managed to avoid the stamp duty imposed by the Government by publishing his newspaper, the *Political Register*, as a pamphlet, thus keeping it at a low price which ensured high circulation figures. He promoted his radical political ideas through his journalism and lecture tours, and gathered together the observations he made on these tours in a collection called *Rural Rides* (1830), which focused on the plight of rural farmers in Britain, interspersing **picturesque** accounts of the countryside with outraged appeals for reform.

Drama

Romantic drama has been the focus of a major reassessment in recent years. Jeffrey N. Cox and Michael Gamer, in their introduction to an anthology of popular plays composed and performed during this time, point to the importance of these shows:

> The theatre was a key meeting point between artists and the public, between aesthetic innovation and popular taste, between the worlds of art and letters and those of commerce and politics. Perhaps more important, it was both the home of spectacularly popular entertainments and the sanctum into which writers most wanted to win their way. (Cox and Gamer 2003: xi)

Cox and Gamer encourage us not to see drama as divorced from the literary pursuits of the writers we have already discussed, not as simply 'low' culture in comparison to them, but as a genre within which the Romantic poets and novelists wished to succeed. Indeed, many of the 'big six' Romantics did write plays, such as Coleridge's *Osario* (1797) and *Remorse* (1812), Wordsworth's *The Borderers* (1796–7), Byron's *The Two Foscari* (1821), and Shelley's *The Cenci* (1819). Byron was on the management sub-committee of one of the two main theatres in London at the time, Drury Lane. Keats declared in an 1819 letter to his publisher, John Taylor, that 'writing a few fine plays' was his 'greatest ambition' (Keats 1959: 294).

Of the plays mentioned, Wordsworth's was rejected by the manager of Covent Garden, the other major theatre in London, and Coleridge's *Osario* by Drury Lane manager Richard Brinsley Sheridan (himself a successful playwright).

Shelley's *The Cenci* had been 'expressly written for theatrical exhibition', written with two famed actors in mind for the two main roles, Edmund Kean and a Miss O'Neil (P. B. Shelley 1964, vol. 2: 102). According to Mary Shelley's later note on the text, the theatre manager of Covent Garden 'pronounced the subject to be so objectionable that he could not even submit the part to Miss O'Neil for perusal' (P. B. Shelley 1970: 337). The 'subject' of the play was incest; the story involves a father raping his daughter, and despite the delicacy with which Shelley thought he had dealt with this subject, the idea of producing such a play could not be countenanced.

This idea that the theatre audience's taste was somehow vulgar has persisted. Evidence is drawn for this argument from the fact that both Drury Lane and Covent Garden were huge, noisy places, where the play performed would be less popular than the pantomimes put on afterwards. These featured such favourites with the public as Grimaldi the Clown and Carlo, the Wonder Dog, whose nightly rescue of a girl drowning during the play *Caravan* (1803) stole the show, or the Harlequin, the silent clown who appeared in *Harlequin and Humpo* (1812). There were prostitutes and beer-sellers competing for the attention of the audience; and between acts and plays (people expected to see more than one play each night) there were magicians, singers and performers more commonly associated now with circuses. Plays could be ruined by the audience's negative reaction, hissing and hollering until it became impossible for the actors to continue.

The notion of the theatre as a less than respectable source of entertainment comes across in the scenes in which the Bertram siblings decide to stage their own performance at home in Austen's *Mansfield Park*. The play they decide upon, *Lovers' Vows*, was a translation and adaption by one-time actress Elizabeth Inchbald of a German drama by August von Koezebue. The inappropriateness of these activities, felt keenly by Fanny Price, probably has more to do with the play's story which exposes the sexual scandal of an aristocrat, Baron Wildenheim, an illegitimate child, and a love affair that crosses a social divide. In practice, such a plot means that characters who are already rather too explicit in their affections for each other can endlessly rehearse scenes which involve both a physical closeness and a declaration of their love for each other. The casting of the play means that two characters can flirt outrageously under the guise of acting. Penny Gay has argued that in the creation of such scenes Austen was drawing attention to the way that social roles, particularly for the upper classes, are performed rather than natural (Gay 2002). Critics have pointed to Austen's own theatre-going and her family's home theatricals as evidence of her enjoyment of the theatre.

One of the foremost playwrights of the period, Joanna Baillie, wrote an 'Introductory Discourse' to *A Series of Plays: In Which it is Attempted to Delineate the Stronger Passions of the Mind* [. . .] (1798) where she set out the attraction of watching drama:

> It is not merely under the violent agitations of passions, that man so rouses and interests us; even the smallest indications of an unquiet mind, the restless eye, the muttering lip, the half-checked exclamation, and the hasty start, will set our attention as anxiously upon the watch as the distant flashes of a gathering storm. (Cox and Gamer 2003: 359)

As this suggests, Baillie's interest is in the passions that we can witness in others, indicated by the slightest gesture or movement. Our fascination with the supernatural, she believed, was based on this. We did not want to see a ghost ourselves but we did want to see a man who believed he had seen one, 'in all the agitation and wildness of that species of terrour [*sic*]' (Cox and Gamer 2003: 359). The plays in this series were intended to delineate particular passions: *Basil* is a tragedy on love, *The Tryal* is a comedy on love, and *De Monfort* a tragedy on hatred. Another kind of drama, known as **'closet drama'**, or the 'theatre of the mind', can be seen in the same light. In Byron's *Manfred*, we see a man being consumed by guilt for a secret he cannot name, which appears to be incest. His deliberations upon suicide and desire for forgetfulness above all things remind us of Johann Wolfgang von Goethe's *Sorrows of Young Werther* (1774), which apparently set the fashion for copycat suicides throughout Europe. In Byron's 'Dramatic Poem', this desire to end his life is matched by Manfred's firmness of mind, and when a demon spirit comes to take him to hell, Faust-like at the end of the play, Manfred refuses to die on any terms but his own. Such Byronic heroes as Manfred reveal the centrality of the dramatic mode in their presentations of the self.

MOVEMENTS AND LITERARY GROUPS

This section introduces a wide range of authors from the period, asking whether the Romantic movement was really made up of solitary male poets at odds with society, and looking at the identifying features of important literary circles, such as the **coteries** of the **Bluestockings**, the Della Cruscan poets, the Warrington academy, the circle surrounding publisher Joseph Johnson in London in the 1790s, the Lake poets, and the 'Cockney School' gathered around Leigh Hunt in the early nineteenth century. While some of these groups were intentionally formed by their members, others were labels given by reviewers or publishers, such as the final group considered here, the peasant-poets.

Outcasts and exiles

Traditionally, the Romantics have been seen as anti-social. This is characterized by the male figure in Caspar David Friedrich's painting, *Wanderer Above a Sea of Mist* (Kunstshalle, Hamburg 1818), who has turned his back on the artist and viewer and stands alone at the top of a mountain, surveying a sublime scene of cloud with a self-assured air and a somewhat proprietorial posture. The male Romantic poet is stereotypically seen as solitary, a man 'not in common with the herd of mankind', as Shelley put it, a comment which reveals his elevated sense of his powers of sensibility and also his rather condescending view of ordinary people (P. B. Shelley 1964, vol. 1: 577). During the Romantic period, poets with radical political views felt they were out of step with the prevalent views of the time. Their unconventional lifestyles, religious beliefs and politics meant that they did not fit into mainstream British society, and both Byron and Shelley lived abroad in self-imposed exile for a significant part of their lives. The rejection they felt was translated into characters such as Manfred, in Byron's dramatic poem of the same name (discussed in the previous section), who feels that his 'Promethean spark' or 'lightning of my being' is 'coop'd in clay', or trapped within and limited by his human body (Norton 2006, vol. 2: 640). Manfred deliberately eschews the company of other men, feeling that when he is with them they bring him down to their level.

This view of Romanticism as 'representing the rejection of Enlightenment sociability' has recently been countered by a collection of essays entitled *Romantic Sociability* (Russell and Tuite 2002). Instead, these essays draw our attention to the socializing that went on among the Romantics, from private dinners in which authors such as Keats and Wordsworth met, to theatre-going, public-lecturing, sonnet-writing competitions at Leigh Hunt's house in Hampstead, suppers given by publishers, and political societies. This new perspective on the period is made possible by the arguments of Jürgen Habermas in his important book, *Structural Transformation of the Public Sphere* (Habermas 1962). Habermas found that in the early eighteenth century the coffee-house culture formed a space for the discussion of politics and news. He argued that through such genres as the epistolary novel what was once private, a letter, moved into the public domain, and this form of 'audience-oriented privacy' continues in the Romantic genre of essays (such as those by William Hazlitt and Charles Lamb), or in the self-dramatization of auto-biography in the **Jacobin** novel (Russell and Tuite 2002: 9). Habermas revealed that an increased sense of investment and engagement in politics showed itself in the periodicals and journals of the period. In reviews of the period's poetry it becomes clear that critics thought about their contemporaries in terms of the network or circle to which they belonged. **Periodicals** such as the *Edinburgh Review* and *Blackwood's Magazine* established groupings through their approbation or criticism of the 'Lake School' to which Wordsworth, Coleridge and Southey belonged, the 'Cockney School' organized around Leigh Hunt – with Keats described disdainfully as a 'Cockney rhymester' – or the 'Satanic School' of Byron and Shelley. In this section, I will examine the ways in which these groups identified themselves and were identified by others as part of literary networks.

Sensibility: from the Bluestockings to the Della Cruscans

Thinking about the social side of Romantic literary circles gives us more information about the female networks in place at these times. One such was the 'Bluestockings', loosely organized around Elizabeth Montagu, the second generation of which included the writers Hannah More and Frances Burney (Haslett 2003). Though this group never constituted itself very strictly as a group, and though they tended to meet privately in each other's houses, it can still be seen as a forum through which women writers engaged in the public sphere, discussing their own and others' writings. The term 'bluestocking' was used pejoratively by male Romantic writers like Byron who, in the first canto of *Don Juan,* ridicules 'the Blues' (Wu 2006: 984). Donna Inez, Don Juan's mother, is a 'learned lady': 'her conversation was obscure / Her thoughts were theorems, her words a problem, / As if she deem'd that mystery would ennoble 'em' (Wu 2006: 940, 941). In fact, the Bluestocking group offered important patronage to emerging female writers, such as the 'peasant poet', the Bristol milkmaid, Ann Yearsley, who was supported by Montagu and More before an acrimonious split over a deed in trust (More had raised funds for Yearsley but wanted to hold it in trust rather than give her the money directly).

More praised the Bluestockings in her poem *The Bas Bleu: Or, Conversation* (1784), which before being published was circulated in manuscript form among the group; in it she remembered the circle of women fondly and praised their conversation as 'Thou bliss of life, and balm of care', which blended 'taste with wit and science' (More 1787).

A number of writers associated with the Bluestockings wrote poems and novels celebrating sensibility, which by this time tended to be linked with women rather than men. Hannah More's poem, 'Sensibility: An Epistle to Mrs Boscawen', was written to another Bluestocking, Frances Boscawen, whose husband Admiral Edward Boscawen had first suggested the circle's name. Sensibility, or the capacity for feeling for others, was believed to be a particularly female characteristic because women's nerves were supposed to be more delicate than men's. More describes sensibility critically in her poem:

> Sweet SENSIBILITY! thou keen delight!
> Unprompted moral! sullen sense of light!
> Perception exquisite! fair virtue's seed!
> Thou quick precursor of the lib'ral deed!
> Thou hasty conscience! reason's blushing morn!
> Instinctive kindness e'er reflection's born!
> Prompt sense of equity! to thee belongs
> The swift redress of unexamin'd wrongs:
> Eager to serve, the cause perhaps untried,
> But always apt to choose the suff'ring side;
> To those who know thee not no words can paint,
> And those who know thee, know all words are faint.
>
> (More 1782)

She describes a kind of instinctive and involuntary generosity of spirit, where a good action is done before it has been thought about. The overriding sense is of one who feels before she reasons, naturally assuming the part or side of those who suffer. This impulsive kindness can easily be criticized. Wrongs are set right ('redressed') swiftly, but these wrongs are also described as 'unexamin'd'; in other words, they are not carefully investigated to find out whether they are truly wrongs. The legal language of a trial continues with the next line in which the 'cause' is served without being tried or judged. Sensibility does not allow time for deliberation or calm meditation; instead, it is the 'quick precursor' of a good deed, the 'prompt sense' of fairness ('equity'), the 'blushing morn' of reason, which again implies an almost involuntary physical reaction. There is also some indication that sensibility is in a sense painful; it is described as a 'keen delight' and as 'exquisite'. Sensibility, particularly an over-refined delicacy of feeling, the poem seems to suggest, can be a burden. Mary Wollstonecraft reserved some of her most scathing criticism for those women who were 'slaves to their bodies' because of such 'artificial notions of beauty, and false descriptions of sensibility' (Wollstonecraft 1997: 157). Elizabeth Carter, another of the Bluestockings, held Rousseau's novel of sensibility, *Julie, ou La Nouvelle Héloïse* (1761), responsible for the affair, and subsequent elopement abroad, of Elizabeth Catherine 'Kitty' Hunter with the tenth Earl of Pembroke, Henry Herbert, who was already married (Barker-Benfield 2001: 108). Lucy Aikin, Anna Barbauld's niece and biographer, told Henry Bright that when *Julie* appeared 'everybody instantly fell in love with everybody', and that this was how 'Mr Barbauld', described elsewhere as an 'unstable Frenchman', 'won his bride' (Janowitz 2002: 70).

Hester Thrale Piozzi, who was the mentor of Fanny Burney and introduced her to the Bluestocking circle, was an important member of another literary group, the so-called Della Cruscans. This group, originally of four poets, met in Italy and published sentimental poetry from Florence, which was well received in England. One member, Robert Merry, found himself famous upon his return to England and began publishing poetry under the pseudonym 'Della Crusca'. His poetry prompted a poetical correspondence between himself and other poets writing under pseudonyms in a journal called *The World*; the playwright Hannah Cowley wrote as 'Anna Matilda', and the poet and one-time actress Mary

Robinson as 'Laura Maria', though others also contributed. The poetical dialogue assumed a passionate and even erotic character as replies were written and published swiftly, with only days between them. Robinson's poem 'Ode to Della Crusca' speaks of an untamed passion; it is a 'wild untutor'd picture of the heart' (Robinson 2000: 87). The poetry produced by the circle promoted displays of apparently unregulated emotion, but it also offended because of its political affiliations, with Merry's support for the French Revolution. Jacqueline Labbe notes that 'Della Cruscan poetry, in its English incarnation, charts a romance in terminology that offends the sensibilities of sensibility: it is too physical, too open, too desiring, too expressive' (Labbe 2000). The critic William Gifford's famous satires on the Della Cruscan poetry, *The Baviad* (1791) and *The Maeviad* (1795), viciously attacked the politics as well as the poetry of this circle, and have been used as evidence of the increasing conservatism of literary taste during the Romantic period.

Anna Barbauld: from the Warrington Academy to London

Anne Janowitz has argued that Anna Barbauld moves between two networks, both centred on her publisher, Joseph Johnson. Barbauld was the daughter of educationalist John Aikin who taught at the Warrington Academy from 1758. The academy was run by **Dissenters** who were unable to hold government office or go to university; some pupils held similar religious beliefs but others were from families who belonged to the Established Church but who thought their sons would gain a better education there. Janowitz argues that the educational methods of the academy influenced Barbauld's poetic style: 'At Warrington tutors aimed to incarnate the ideal of social intercourse conceived of as informal, familiar and amiable, teaching the virtues of "candid manners" and an "active mind"' (Janowitz 2002: 62). The poems in Barbauld's first collection, *Poems* (1773), published before she was married and under her maiden name Anna

Aikin, show the kind of sociability that was encouraged by
the academy. These poems are often written as though to an
intimate companion in a conversational style that would later
become associated with Coleridge (see the earlier discussion
of his conversational poems). The Dissenters were a close-
knit community, bound by ties of faith and a recognition that
they were rejected by society, though they also felt that they
were on the verge of gaining political rights. The Test and
Corporations Act would be repealed in 1828 (see Chapter 1,
Religion and Philosophy); it perhaps took longer for this to
happen because of the very public support that prominent
Dissenters gave to the French Revolution. Janowitz argues
that their inability to hold public office gave them a moral
high-ground from which to comment on political matters,
since they could not be corrupted. For part of the time that
Barbauld lived at the academy, the natural philosopher
Joseph Priestley was also a tutor; for him science was inextri-
cable from radical politics (for more on Priestley see the
section on Science and Technology in the previous chapter).
Deirdre Coleman has argued that Barbauld set herself the
task of trying to 'soften and temper Priestley's masculine
rigour', his 'philistinism' and 'rough and unamiable rationality [which] sometimes seemed at odds with the habits of
social existence' (Coleman 2002: 84, 88, 91). Many of
Barbauld's poems in her first collection evoke scenes of
domestic happiness with an ideal circle of family and friends.
There are poems directly addressed to those in the
Warrington Academy, for example 'To Mrs. P___, With
Some Drawings of Birds and Insects', addressed to Mary
Priestley. Barbauld writes that 'friendship, better than a Muse
inspires' (Barbauld 1773).

In 'The Invitation', published in *Poems*, Barbauld portrays
the Warrington Academy as a place that encourages a 'proud
disdain of interest's sordid bribe', where, in the true
Enlightenment sense, the 'gentlest arts and purest manners'
meet (Barbauld 1773). Unafraid of making a political statement, she refers to the 'bigot rage' against religious Non-
Conformists that has retarded the advancement of science:

Here nature opens all her secret springs,
And heav'n-born science plumes her eagle wings:
Too long has bigot rage, with malice swell'd,
Crush'd her strong pinions, and her flight withheld.

(Barbauld 1773)

Barbauld's poems had circulated in manuscript within her circle before her brother persuaded her to publish them, which suggests she had a supportive coterie of friends at Warrington. They were received with great acclaim, going into a fifth edition by 1777. Barbauld therefore entered the public arena as one of a defined group and promoted their ideals, but once there she was also encouraged by others, such as the Bluestockings. More's poem 'Sensibility', for example, identifies Barbauld by name, as 'much-loved' (Wu 2006: 58).

Reviews of Barbauld's *Poems* reveal that appreciation was very much grounded in a clear sense of distinction between the sexes:

> This Lady is not only *poetically enchanting*, but personally attractive. With a countenance in which every thing agreeable in a woman is strongly expressed, she prepossesses you extremely in her favour at first sight; and you are doubly pleased with the display of her intellectual powers in conversation with her, as she seems not to be conscious of an understanding superior to the greatest part of her sex. (Anon. 1776)

There is a deal of emphasis here on Barbauld's supposed character, as imagined by the (probably male) reviewer. He describes the encounter with her through her poems as like meeting her, and he imagines reading in her countenance 'every thing agreeable in a woman', enjoying her conversation and particularly appreciating her modesty in not acknowledging her superior powers to other women (he does not, of course, suggest that she might excel in her understanding when compared to members of the other sex). The metaphors propose a kind of physical and perhaps even

erotic encounter. She is found to be '*enchanting*', suggesting
the allure of the exotic while offering a rather patronizing
compliment. In fact, the opening poem of her *Poems* was
'Corsica', and was addressed to the island, described as 'The
fort of freedom', in admiration of its efforts to win political
independence from France.

In 1774, Barbauld married Rochemont Barbauld and
moved to London, but remained within a circle of friends and
family who shared political and religious beliefs, including
Mary Wollstonecraft. However, Barbauld did not seem to
think of herself within a specifically female community, such
as the Bluestockings did. For example, when she was asked by
Elizabeth Montagu to start an academy for women, Barbauld
refused, claiming that 'the best way for a woman to acquire
knowledge is from conversation with a father or brother'
(cited in Janowitz 2004: 18). Instead, Barbauld set up a school
for boys with her husband when she first moved south to
Palgrave in Suffolk. Barbauld's views on women's rights are
difficult to fathom, and she seems not to have shared
Wollstonecraft's more explicit feminism. The latter declared
that an 'ignoble comparison' was made between women and
flowers in one of Barbauld's poems published in 1773, 'To a
Lady, With Some Painted Flowers' (Wollstonecraft 1997:
168). In this poem, Barbauld writes that the 'fair' Lady copies
the flowers in two senses of the word. Both that she represents
them in her painting but also that she imitates them in her
ability to please others. Just as flowers 'spring to cheer the
sense, and glad the heart', so the Lady's 'best' and 'sweetest
empire is – to please' (Barbauld 1773). Wollstonecraft
objected because such language 'robs the whole sex of its
dignity and classes the brown and fair [women] with the
smiling flowers that only adorn the land' (Wollstonecraft
1997: 167–8).

Barbauld kept a strict idea of the division between the
sexes, while Wollstonecraft was less convinced of a 'supposed
sexual character'; in other words, she believed the difference
between men and women was socially constructed rather
than anything natural (Wollstonecraft 1997: 168). While

both Barbauld and Wollstonecraft moved in the same circles in the late 1780s, and while they shared radical political views in some regards, their views of gender were clearly different. Both were published by Joseph Johnson, a Unitarian who employed William Blake as an engraver and also published the writers Erasmus Darwin and William Godwin (discussed in the previous chapter). Johnson's authors regularly attended suppers at his house and a radical circle emerged; Wollstonecraft first met her future husband, Godwin, at one of Johnson's dinners, where Tom Paine was also present. Perhaps influenced by this new circle in London, Barbauld's political voice grew stronger and more determined, resulting finally in her poem *Eighteen Hundred and Eleven, A Poem*, in which she called for an end to the war with France. The almost universal disapproval for this work, often coupled with malicious reference to the unseemliness of a woman speaking of such things, put an end to Barbauld's poetic career. John Wilson Croker's offended tone in the *Quarterly Review* poured sarcasm on her poetic attempt to intervene in the country's political affairs: 'We had hoped, indeed, that the empire might have been saved without the intervention of a lady-author' (Wu 2006: 34).

The English Jacobins

Godwin's circle in London in the 1790s included S. T. Coleridge, Humphry Davy, Mary Hays, William Hazlitt, Thomas Holcroft, John and Charles Kemble, Charles Lamb, John Thelwall, Elizabeth Inchbald, Richard Brinsley Sheridan and Helen Maria Williams. Many of these writers were associated by their support of the ideals for the French Revolution. Williams, for example, was a poet of sensibility who wrote anti-slavery poetry and became involved in the campaign to get the Test and Corporations Acts repealed, but she is now best known for her series *Letters from France* (1790–6), which described her experiences in France in the years immediately following the Revolution. Gary Kelly has defined a new genre of literature produced by certain of

Godwin's circle at this time, which he calls the 'coterie novel': 'The coterie novel was derived from forms that had long been in use but that underwent rapid elaboration and intense application during the Revolution debate of the late eighteenth and early nineteenth century' (Kelly 2000: 147). Kelly argues that this sub-genre is particularly associated with the circles to which Wollstonecraft and Mary Shelley belonged, the former in the 1790s and the latter in the 1810s, and that it was deliberately developed to represent the ideals of their circle, or 'coterie', to the public. An important concept when considering the many, distinctive literary groups and movements of the period, Kelly defines a coterie as 'a group of personally acquainted individuals, meeting informally and corresponding with each other, who advance certain shared social, cultural or political interests' (Kelly 2000: 148). The link for many of these particular writers was France: Williams lived in France for most of her life and wrote eyewitness accounts of her time there from her first visit in the summer of 1790; Thomas Christie went to Paris in 1790 and returned there in 1792; and Wollstonecraft joined his circle when she went there in December 1792. They were closely associated with the **Girondins**, who were a loosely formed political grouping that were arrested and executed during the Terror (Kelly 2000: 148).

Kelly argues that on her return to England, Wollstonecraft became involved in a concerted effort to form a coterie based on similar principles to those of the Girondins, but their efforts to achieve political reform were made through literature. Like the Girondins, the Godwin circle 'attempted to live out their revolutionary principles in daily conjugal, domestic, and private life' (Kelly 2000: 149). In turn, they made themselves and their lives the subject of their literary works. Wollstonecraft's novel, *The Wrongs of Woman, or, Maria* (1798), can be read autobiographically, commenting on the author's romantic sensibilities and failed relationships. These writers, then, self-consciously identified themselves as a group but they were also pejoratively identified as such by reviewers and their audiences, in particular labelled as Jacobins by the

Anti-Jacobin Review, which was founded by the Tory politician George Canning. This is one of a number of instances discussed in this chapter where a literary group or movement was in part defined by those in opposition to its political beliefs. The act of labelling writers such as Godwin, Wollstonecraft and Inchbald as Jacobins had the effect of making them appear a far more organized threat than they actually were, and ignored the range of responses offered in their writings. The presentation of these writers as a coherent group indicates an attempt on their enemies' part to create factions, and the 'English Jacobins' were characterized as anti-patriotic. In turn, there were novels which can be labelled 'anti-Jacobin', published as part of a larger campaign to defend hierarchy against the challenge of demands for equality, such as Robert Bisset's *Douglas; Or, The Highlander* (1800) in which Mary Wollstonecraft is parodied as Lady Mary Manhunt (see Grenby 2001).

Periodicals and 'The Lakers'

Literary groups, then, were in part self-defining and in part defined by others, particularly by the reviewers of the period. Reviews had become more important because far more books were now being published. From the early nineteenth century, two major periodicals, the *Edinburgh Review* and the *Quarterly Review*, began to publish substantial reviews. These were not just the brief advertisements for books that had been seen in periodicals previously but reviews which had ideological positions to uphold and to attack. These two periodicals developed in opposition to each other just as the *Critical Review* had been set up in opposition to the *Monthly Review* in the mid-1700s. Respectively, these occupied the two major opposing political perspectives, labelled as Tory and Whig. Tories were characterized by their desire to maintain the status quo and deny calls for reform and religious toleration; the Whigs tended to be more liberal and progressive.

Francis Jeffrey was the editor of the *Edinburgh Review* for 27 years; he was a Whig in his politics and would become a

Scottish judge and MP. From the outset, the *Edinburgh Review* tried to distinguish itself from other similar publications, declaring that it would select from the books published rather than attempting to cover them all; by 1818, it had attained a circulation of nearly 14,000. Reviewers often used their reviews as an excuse to advance their own literary tastes. One of Jeffrey's early targets was the 'Lake School', a term he created for the 'sect' of poets that included Coleridge, Southey and Wordsworth and who lived in the Lake District in the North of England. In his article on Southey's *Thalaba, the Destroyer* (1801), Jeffrey pronounced Southey 'one of the chief champions and apostles' of this sect (Jeffrey 1802: 63). He criticized the project of the Lake School for its 'representation of vulgar manners, in vulgar language', and Southey's poetry for being 'often puerile, diffuse, and artificial' (Jeffrey 1802: 67, 83). These terms recur often in his hounding of the 'Lakers', as Byron called them in the Dedication to *Don Juan* (Wu 2006: 933). In Jeffrey's later review of Wordsworth's *Poems, in Two Volumes* (1807), he again dismissed the 'brotherhood of poets' who have long been 'labouring to establish' their 'school of poetry' (Jeffrey 1807: 214). He criticized the *Lyrical Ballads* for its 'occasional vulgarity, affectation and silliness' (Jeffrey 1807: 214).

Wordsworth was to live in Grasmere, in the Lake District, for 14 years, and in 1810 first published a version of his *Guide through the District of the Lakes in the North of England, with a Description of the Scenery, &c. for the Use of Tourists and Residents.* This guidebook was the most read of all of his writings, and was republished a number of times during his lifetime. In it, Wordsworth wrote of the changes that had occurred since the rise in the numbers of tourists and settlers. He urged people to protect the landscape that he had loved since he was a boy, and because of this, his work has been seen as presenting an 'ecological view of the natural world' (McKusick 2005: 202). James McKusick argues that the poetry of Coleridge and Wordsworth 'consistently expresses a deep and abiding interest in the Earth as a dwelling place for all living things' (McKusick 2005: 202). As Thomas de Quincey wrote to Wordsworth: 'Your name is with me forever linked to the lovely scenes of nature' (Wu 2006: 806).

In 'Ode: Intimations of Immortality from Recollections of Early Childhood' (1807), Wordsworth remembers 'a time when meadow, grove, and stream, / The earth, and every common sight' had 'The glory and the freshness of a dream' (Norton 2006, vol. 2: 308). He feels that this 'visionary gleam' has left him, now that he is older, but he is still capable of an intense feeling of belonging and love for the land: 'I love the Brooks which down their channels fret, / Even more than when I tripped lightly as they' (Norton 2006, vol. 2: 308, 312). Another Lake poet, despite the fact that she was not published within her lifetime, was William's sister Dorothy, who kept a diary between 1800 and 1803 while they lived in Grasmere, and Coleridge lived 13 miles away in Keswick. This diary is full of natural detail, as well as recording the lives of the poor who travelled through or lived in the Lakes. Many of the scenes recorded find their way into Wordsworth's and Coleridge's poetry, and they show Dorothy's love for the Lakes and its inhabitants. In a poem called 'Grasmere – A Fragment', she recalls a time when she had just arrived there, and was yet 'A Stranger, Grasmere, in thy Vale' (Norton 2006, vol. 2: 403). She discovers in the hills one that is covered in colourful mosses, various trees and vegetation and concludes: 'No more I'll grieve: for Winter here / Hath pleasure of his own' (Norton 2006, vol. 2: 404). This realization is accompanied by the sound of a stream that seemed to tell her to 'Rejoice!' By the end of the poem she no longer considers herself a stranger but 'an Inmate of this vale' (Norton 2006, vol. 2: 404). In both Wordsworths' writings there is a distinct and passionate sense of place and of belonging to the Lakes.

As William Wordsworth's fame as a poet grew, and his guidebook became well known, more tourists and well-wishers flocked to the Lakes to visit him. In 1809, de Quincey moved to Grasmere and became the new tenant of the Wordsworths' home, Dove Cottage. He would eventually publish his *Recollections of the Lake Poets* (1839–40), describing the circle in intimate detail. One essay, first published as

'Lake Reminiscences' in *Tait's Edinburgh Magazine* (1839), records a long walk he and Wordsworth took during the Peninsular War at midnight 'to meet the carrier who brought the London newspapers by a circuitous course from Keswick' (Wu 2006: 823). The essay presents a lifelike Wordsworth, in a mundane and ordinary situation, but also endeavours to correct critics' misunderstanding of Wordsworth's poem 'There was a boy'. Unfortunately, relations had soured between de Quincey and the Lakers by this date and the publication of these memoirs further distanced them, with Wordsworth declaring 'I have never read a word of his infamous production, nor ever shall' (Wu 2006: 809).

The Cockney School and Keats

Jeffrey N. Cox has shown that many of the same phrases and grounds for criticism were used in the notorious attacks on another school of poets, the so-called 'Cockney School' gathered around Leigh Hunt, and extended to include Byron, Hazlitt, Keats, Charles Lamb and Percy Shelley. Cox points out that the first attack on this new threat in *Blackwood's Edinburgh Magazine* (1817) actually defines one school by its opposition to the other:

> While the whole critical world is occupied with balancing the merits, whether in theory or in execution of what is commonly called THE LAKE SCHOOL, it is strange that no one seems to think it at all necessary to say a single word about another new school of poetry which has of late sprung up among us . . . it may henceforth be referred to by the designation of THE COCKNEY SCHOOL. (cited by Cox 1999)

The series of essays begun by this article were written by the editors of *Blackwood's Edinburgh Magazine*, John Gibson Lockhart and John Wilson Croker, who, as Nicholas Roe has pointed out, 'were in no doubt about the malign effect of their essays on the reputations of Keats, Hunt, and Hazlitt' (Roe 1997: 12). Roe quotes an 1818 letter from Croker and

Lockhart to the publisher John Murray in which they rev-
elled in their creation of 'that happy name which you & all
the reviewers are now borrowing – *the Cockney School* – a thorn
which will stick to them & madden them & finally damn
them' (Roe 1997: 12). Though written in defence of Keats,
Shelley's attack on the *Quarterly Review's* 'savage criticism' of
Keats's *Endymion* helped to fulfil Croker and Lockhart's
prophecy (Wu 2006: 1200). In response to an article written
by Croker in the April 1818 issue of the *Quarterly Review*,
Shelley portrayed Keats as weak, his genius 'not less delicate
and fragile as it was beautiful':

> The savage criticism on his *Endymion*, which appeared in the
> *Quarterly Review*, produced the most violent effect on his suscep-
> tible mind; the agitation thus originated ended in the rupture of
> a blood-vessel in the lungs; a rapid consumption ensued, and the
> succeeding acknowledgements from more candid critics of the
> true greatness of his powers, were ineffectual to heal the wound
> thus wantonly inflicted. (Wu 2006: 1200)

Shelley's sympathy in describing Keats thus can be contrasted with Byron's rather more cynical claim that Keats had
been 'snuff'd out by an article' (Byron 1986, vol. 5: 483).
Long-lasting damage was done to Keats's reputation by the
well-meaning and malicious alike: Roe has argued that the
'mischief of the "Cockney School" essays was virulent, and
has endured to the present time' (Roe 1997: 11).

Greg Kucich lists a number of characteristics used to iden-
tify the 'Cockney School of Poetry' and traces them back to
Hunt's political and poetic objectives. Kucich describes how
conservative reviewers, such as 'Z', were 'appalled by the
diabolical blend of Jacobinism, radical aesthetic experimen-
tation, and erotic license promulgated in Hunt circle writings' (Kucich 2004: 266). This can be seen in Keats's poetry
particularly, in the radical eroticism of such poems as *The Eve
of St Agnes* (1820), with its sensuality and use of feminine
rhymes (rhyming on the penultimate syllable). It is a romance
of the medieval kind, set in a castle during Catholic times,

sharing similarities with Hunt's chivalric romance, *Story of Rimini* (1816). Both poems feature lovers separated by forces beyond their control and a kind of pervading 'gloominess', which Kucich argues is characteristic of the texts produced by these second-generation writers who found themselves in a world in which the French Revolution and hopes for reform in Britain had failed and where the greatest literary hopes had turned into political apostates. By this time, Southey was Poet Laureate, writing verses in praise of the Government, and Wordsworth had accepted a government post. As Kucich argues, once considered as part of the Hunt 'lineage', Keats's poems 'do not aspire to escapist fantasy but rather emanate from material social conditions and strategic imaginative procedures for effecting political change in a gloomy world' (Kucich 2004: 274).

Kucich also emphasizes the coterie nature of this circle, who read each other's poetry in manuscript form, corrected texts and saw them through the printing process, and even collaborated on certain projects, such as Percy and Mary Shelley's jointly authored *History of a Six Weeks' Tour* (1817). Some relationships have been subject to more critical attention than others, most particularly the relationships between Byron and Percy Shelley and between Mary and Percy Shelley; in both, one writer has been seen as either enabling or strangling the creativity of the other. Instead, it is possible to read the writings of the Shelleys and Byron as in dialogue with each other. *Frankenstein, or, The Modern Prometheus* (1818) might be said to offer a critique of the solipsism and defiance of the Prometheus figure found in Byron's poem of that name, and in Shelley's *Prometheus Unbound*, a figure that Byron and Shelley clearly identified with but whom Mary Shelley negatively linked with the overreaching Victor Frankenstein. Shelley's 'Julian and Maddalo' presents discussions between Shelley, disguised as the 'rather serious' Julian, and Byron, the despondent and proud Count Maddalo (P. B. Shelley 1977: 113). Countering Maddalo's accusation, 'You talk Utopia', Julian answers with a faith in human suffering and endurance: it is possible to see in this encounter Shelley's conviction that change can be effected and Byron's misanthropy and gloominess. These positions were parodied in Thomas Love Peacock's novels, such as *Nightmare Abbey* (1818), where Mr Cypress represents Byron and Scythrop is a portrayal of Shelley.

The coterie was such that Mary Shelley would later describe herself as 'the last relic of a beloved race' (M. Shelley 1987: 456–7). In her novel *The Last Man* (1826), she idealizes their circle in the portrayal of Adrian (Shelley), Raymond (Byron) and their community. The society described in this novel, which is set in the future, is a republican one, but this is destroyed by the final leveller, a plague that wipes out the human population. The political change that Percy Shelley wished for his entire life therefore comes, in Mary Shelley's novel, at a terrible cost. Even in this portrayal, Mary Shelley critiques the optimism of her now dead companions; John Williams has argued that the portraits of Shelley and Byron reveal 'flawed' characters and 'what Mary Shelley writes is in the end an uncompromising denial of the Shelleyan ideal' (Williams 2000: 113, 114). Such works as this and de Quincey's *Recollections of the Lake Poets* remember and celebrate literary, political and intellectual circles that are now in the past, while also critiquing them.

Labouring-class poets

Where the 'Cockney School' was defined as such by its opponents, other labels were given to writers by their supporters. The final literary group I shall consider here was more the product of publishers than the poets themselves. The term 'labouring class' was used in a kind of marketing ploy by publishers, and the reputations of such Romantic poets as John Clare and Robert Bloomfield have particularly been shaped by this title. Recent work by John Goodridge and others has resulted in a database of British and Irish labouring-class poets who lived and worked between 1700 and 1900, and in an edition of their work (Goodridge 2006). In general, the term is used to refer to writers being at least partially, if not wholly, self-taught. Some poets are identified by occupation, such as the shoe-makers and weavers, geographical location or political agenda. Goodridge points out that these labels were used to present authors in a particular way, to package them as 'novelties'. He makes links with other poets, such as the poet and forger Thomas Chatterton who committed suicide aged 17, who were similarly presented as 'precocious youths' (Goodridge 2006). Chatterton was heralded by Wordsworth in 'Resolution and Independence' (1807) as 'the marvellous Boy' unable to cope with the 'despondency and madness' that comes with poetic genius (Norton 2006, vol. 2: 303).

In 'Resolution and Independence', Wordsworth also praised Robert Burns (1759–96), in effect characterizing him as a labouring-class poet: 'Him who walked in glory and in joy / Following his plough, along the mountain-side' (Norton 2006, vol. 2: 303). Burns had promoted himself in this manner; his *Poems, Chiefly in the Scottish Dialect* (1787) carried an anonymous dedication to the 'Simple Bard! unbroke by rules of Art!', and his poetry is described as 'wild effusions' that have been inspired by nature alone (Burns 1786: iv). In the Preface to his collection, Burns describes how he has composed this poetry 'amid the toils and fatigues of a laborious life' and asks his readers, 'particularly the Learned and the Polite', to 'make every allowance for Education and Circumstances of Life' (Burns 1786: iv, vi). It seems that his disclaimer did the trick because his *Poems* sold out within a month of being published, and reviews signalled the approbation of the 'Learned and Polite'. The *New London Magazine* declared that it had never before 'met with a more signal instance of true and uncultivated genius than in the author of these poems' (cited by Wu 2006: 261). Soon, Burns was being described by the Scottish novelist Henry Mackenzie as the 'heaven-taught ploughman'. Burns's verse was written in Scots dialect, which encouraged an understanding of him as untutored, but such a judgement underestimated his radical agenda. Even by using this vernacular in his poetry, Burns was aligning himself with a tradition of Scottish verse, such as the poetry of Allan Ramsay and Robert Fergusson, influenced by folk ballads and songs. In 'Epistle to J. L*****k, an old Scotch bard, 1 April 1785', Burns praises a song by the farmer-poet, John Lapraik, which 'thirled the heart strings through the breast' (Wu 2006: 262). When he hears the song, Burns wonders who could have written it, but finds that it is not written by 'Pope and Steele / Or Beattie', but instead 'an odd kind chiel', or man, from 'About Murkirk', a village in Scotland (Wu 2006: 262).

As Fiona Stafford has argued, 'despite the apparent humility of the preface, Burns's collection of poems challenges pretty much every kind of contemporary authority – linguistic, clerical, aristocratic, even monarchical' (Stafford 2005: 119). Burns's poetry was deliberately regional and often witty; and its colloquial, conversational style appealed to Wordsworth, who would also argue for naturalness in poetry. Burns's politics, influenced not only by Scottish nationalism but also by the writings of Richard Price and Tom Paine, can be seen in such poems as 'To a Mouse, on turning her up in her nest, with the plough, November 1785'. In this poem, Burns laments that 'man's dominion / Has broken nature's social union': the mouse can no longer see man as his 'earthborn companion' and 'fellow mortal!' (Wu 2006: 268). Despite his protestations that his verse was 'rude an' rough', his muse was 'hamely [homely] in attire', and that he had 'to learning nae pretence', Burns's writing was highly sophisticated, displaying knowledge of the classical traditions of English poetry as well as Scottish ('Epistle to J. L*****k [. . .]', Wu 2006: 263–4). In style, Burns is an important predecessor of John Clare, who was similarly influenced by these literary traditions, as well as by oral traditions of singing and verse-making.

Clare was promoted as the 'Northamptonshire Peasant Poet' but found that this label was often more constricting than beneficial. Lockhart, in his anonymous review of Keats, had referred to the labouring-class poetry of his time as the 'most incurable' of the 'manias of our mad age': 'The just celebrity of Robert Burns and Miss Baillie has had the melancholy effect of turning the heads of we know not how many farm-servants and unmarried ladies' (Wu 2006: 1327). This 'mania' went further back than Burns – for example, to literary gentlemen such as Joseph Spence, an Oxford Professor of Poetry, who scoured rural areas for poets to patronize earlier in the eighteenth century (Goodridge and Keegan 2004). Ann Yearsley has already been mentioned in this chapter; she was described by her patron, Hannah More, as 'a Milker of Cows, and a feeder of Hogs, who has never even *seen* a Dictionary' (cited by Haslett 2004: 54). Robert Bloomfield's first collection of poems was published under the title *A Farmer's Boy* in 1800, and the name was soon used to refer to Bloomfield himself. As many of these writers found, success was brief and the myth of the 'untutored genius', a phrase used by Southey in an essay appended to his publication of *An Attempt in Verse, by John Jones, an Old Servant* in 1831, ended in a return to poverty and an early death. Chatterton, born and educated in the mercantile city of Bristol, is obviously also part of this lineage.

Clare wished to merge labouring-class poetry with other English literary traditions, but found the polite, literary, metropolitan world resistant to his experiments in high art, preferring the vernacular Northamptonshire dialect and typical labouring-class subjects. Even the vogue for this waned as the nineteenth century went on. Clare's first volume of verse was successful but later collections were not; Clare had to return to farm labour and eventually lived out his days in Northampton General Lunatic Asylum. His work is characterized by an intense sense of place and displacement. This is shown in his poems about Helpstone, the village in which he was born and in which he knew every tree individually. When he moved only three miles from Helpstone, he recorded the painful upheaval in 'The Flitting': his new home he considered full of 'All foreign things' (Wu 2006: 1232). In 'I am', a poem written in the misery of his mental illness, he declares his displacement from himself: 'I am – yet what I am, none cares or knows' (Wu 2006: 1237). The grouping together of labouring-class poets is in many respects an artificial one and yet it is a group that was identi-fied as such during the Romantic period; Goodridge and Bridget Keegan warn against a critical tendency to ghettoize such writers, but also acknowledge that they themselves con-sciously wrote within a labouring-class tradition (Goodridge and Keegan 2004: 293).

3

Critical Approaches

Historical Overview
Current Issues and Debates

INTRODUCTION

This chapter will begin by looking at definitions given by Romantic-period writers themselves of how they characterized their own age. It also looks at notions which we now consider characteristically Romantic, such as Wordsworth's 'spots of time', S. T. Coleridge's and Percy Shelley's ideas of the imagination, and Thomas Love Peacock's criticism of poetry in *The Four Ages of Poetry*. The chapter then briefly surveys the change in critical approaches to the Romantic period, from the Victorians' view of the Romantics, the canonization of, for example, Wordsworth's poetry, and the pre-Raphaelite sanitizing of Keats and Shelley, to the Modernists' distaste for all things Romantic. Looking here at T. E. Hulme's writings on Romanticism, it is possible to discern more about the period criticizing than that being criticized. In many respects, Romantic writers such as Shelley continued to be out of favour with critics well into the twentieth century – for example, with critics such as T. S. Eliot and F. R. Leavis. This chapter then considers twentieth-century critics whose work has affected Romanticism particularly, such as M. H. Abrams,

Geoffrey Hartman, and, briefly, Harold Bloom and Northrop Frye.

HISTORICAL OVERVIEW

Definitions of Romanticism

None of the writers discussed in this book would have considered themselves 'Romantics'. This is a term that was assigned to them by a later generation and in this section I consider how they have been thought of since the time in which they were writing. It is important to note, however, that there was a definite sense during the period I have been calling 'Romantic' that something different was happening, a genuine break from the past. The first example that the *Oxford English Dictionary* gives of the term 'Romanticism', defined as the 'distinctive qualities or spirit of the romantic school in art, literature, and music', occurs in a quotation from *The New Monthly Magazine* in 1823: 'The French Academy . . . has determined never to receive within its bosom any one polluted by the dramatic heresy of romanticism.' The *Oxford English Dictionary* then points the reader to a definition of 'Classicism', since it is in opposition to this movement that Romanticism is first defined. Lady Morgan (pen-name Sydney Owenson) is also quoted discussing the novel *Cinq Mars* (1826) by Alfred de Vigny: 'In the composition of Cinq Mars, there is none of the exaggeration or pedantrie of romanticism or of classicism' (*Oxford English Dictionary*). Here 'exaggeration' refers to 'romanticism' and 'pedantrie' to 'classicism'; these two terms are held in contrast to each other, the first implying a wilful overabundance and the second implying discipline. From the outset, then, Romanticism is defined in negative terms, implying a disease that pollutes and corrupts in one quotation and a lack of discipline in the other. It is interesting, too, that these qualities are associated with national difference in both quotations; though the scope of this book only deals with British literature and the culture of the period, European Romanticism offers a very different interpretation and timescale (see Bode 2005: 126–36).

There were a number of important texts written by contemporary writers themselves that attempt to define what they saw as their project, many of which have since become foundations for an understanding of the critical and cultural entity that is called Romanticism. Wordsworth's Preface to the 1802 edition of the *Lyrical Ballads* (also discussed in the previous chapter) is one such text. The Preface positively encourages the 'spontaneous overflow of powerful feeling' in poetry, and Wordsworth's own poetry is often used as an example of this new emphasis on self-expression (p. 242). Indeed, the Preface was written as an attempt to justify his poetic endeavours; and his long autobiographical poem *The Prelude*, which he revised throughout his life and which was only published posthumously, was given the subtitle *Growth of a Poet's Mind*. This poem was about Wordsworth himself, how he had developed as a poet, and the experiences that had formed him; more philosophically, it explored the mind's constant revision of memories which are often linked to powerful emotions. In *The Prelude* he identified a number of 'spots of time' which are important to us in explaining who we now are, and which, when we remember them, have a 'renovating virtue' on our minds, continuing to nourish and repair us in times of need (XII, ll. 208, 210). This new determination to make the mind the subject of study is one possible definition of Romanticism, but it is one that Keats labelled the 'egotistical sublime' (as discussed in Chapter 2), and clearly it does not apply to all writers of the period (Norton 2006, vol. 2: 947). *The Prelude* was published in 1850, the same year as Tennyson's elegy *In Memoriam, A. H. H.* Tennyson's poem was a far greater success, and it took a long time for Wordsworth's poem to be appreciated critically. Duncan Wu accounts for this in the following way: 'The story [*The Prelude*] tells – of promise under constant threat; of a man scarred by loss; of a poetic sensibility and its long, arduous journey to maturity – is of our own time' (Wu 2006: 416). Wordsworth's reputation fluctuated throughout the nineteenth and twentieth centuries, but he is very much the most canonized Romantic in the present day, taught on most university programmes.

The Romantic imagination

Samuel Taylor Coleridge wrote his *Biographia Literaria* (1817) when the friendship between himself and Wordsworth had waned, and in some respects it is an attempt by Coleridge to set down his recollections of their earlier collaboration. It is far more important as a critical text in its own right, presenting Coleridge's argument concerning the central importance of the imagination to his work and thought. In this regard, it is a manifesto for another type of Romanticism than that offered by Wordsworth, one that was particularly resonant for the New Critics of the twentieth century. New Criticism was the dominant form of critical approach from the 1920s to the 1960s; it emphasized the text itself rather than its social, political or cultural context. Some Romantics fared better than others with the New Critics; Keats, for example, was admired by Cleanth Brooks in his 1947 book *The Well Wrought Urn: Studies in the Structure of Poetry* and Coleridge's metaphors for the imagination, that it is organic and has a synthesizing power, appealed to the New Critical idea of unity within poetry. In particular, these critics appreciated the idea that form and content would reflect each other and that the poem could be a self-sufficient whole without need for recourse to either authorial intention or reader response; meaning was to be found in the text and the text alone. Coleridge described the imagination's agency using the following metaphor:

> It dissolves, diffuses, dissipates, in order to re-create; or where this process is rendered impossible, yet still at all events it struggles to idealize and to unify. It is essentially *vital*, even as all objects (*as objects*) are essentially fixed and dead. (Wu, 2006: 692)

This idea of the imagination as 'essentially *vital*' resurfaces in Cleanth Brooks's understanding of the 'interior life of the poem' (cited in Leitch 2001: 1351). In Coleridge, poetry is compared to an organic being, which develops according to this 'interior life'.

Percy Shelley's *A Defence of Poetry* also emphasized the active nature of the imagination, describing poetry as 'vitally metaphorical' (P. B. Shelley 1977: 482). He made a distinction between two different operations of the mind, two different processes of thought: reason and the imagination. Reason he described as the 'mind contemplating the relations borne by one thought to another', whereas imagination is the 'mind acting on those thoughts so as to colour them with its own light, and composing from them [. . .] other thoughts' (P. B. Shelley 1977: 480). In the first the mind is 'contemplating'; in the second the mind is 'acting'. In other words, reason is reflective and contemplative while the imagination is active. He continues, describing the imagination as a principle of synthesis which draws things together; reason, on the other hand, is a principle of analysis which simply sees the relations between things without attempting to synthesize the things thus related. Where reason simply details or lists quantities already known, the imagination perceives the value of these quantities; where reason respects differences between things, imagination respects similitude between them. This can be likened to Coleridge's idea of the imagination, which is creative by means of harmony and synthesis. Shelley's use of the adverb 'vitally' also recalls Coleridge's terms similarly drawn from biology. In the *Defence*, Shelley writes that without the application of abstract ideas to new historical and political contexts, without seeing and expressing new similarity or relation between things, language would be 'dead' (P. B. Shelley 1977: 482).

Anti-Romantic writing

Percy Shelley wrote *A Defence of Poetry* in answer to his friend Thomas Love Peacock's essay *The Four Ages of Poetry*, which was published in 1820. Shelley's *Defence* was not published until 1840, well after his death, but it is important to remember that he was responding to this specific text. Peacock argues that there are four ages of poetry: iron (the days of 'bards' and 'warriors'), golden ('the age of Homer' and the ancient Greeks), silver (the age of Roman poets, such as Horace and Juvenal) and brass (which began with the medieval period and in which he includes his own age). He sees the origins of poetry in bards singing the triumphs of their chieftains after they have been paid in 'liquor' (Peacock 2001: 685–9). Poetry is 'like all other trades', it takes 'its rise in the demand for the commodity, and flourishes in proportion to the extent of the market' (Peacock 2001: 685). This argument is part of Peacock's attempt to bring poets back down to earth; he does not think they should have such exalted notions of themselves. In his scathing attack on the poets of his age, we can see a very modern notion of the poet as a 'waster of his own time' (Peacock 2001: 694).

Peacock also asserts that within the 'brass period', there have been four ages of poetry, and the poetry we would call 'Romantic' represents the brass (and therefore most inferior) period of that. He is particularly vicious in his attack on the Lake Poets, pretending to mimic them with these words:

> Poetic impressions can be received only among natural scenes: for all that is artificial is anti-poetical. Society is artificial, therefore we will live out of society. The mountains are natural, therefore we will live in the mountains. There we shall be shining models of purity and virtue, passing the whole day in the innocent and amiable occupation of going up and down hill, receiving poetical impressions, and communicating them in immortal verse to admiring generations. (Peacock 2001: 692)

He attacks poets for thinking themselves superior to others, for cutting themselves off from society and writing only about nature, and for being self-obsessed. Peacock claimed that the inspirations of poetry can never make a 'useful or a rational man' (Peacock 2001: 693). This notion of what it means to be a 'Romantic' has persisted and Peacock at least thinks there is some truth in it. He describes Wordsworth as a 'morbid dreamer', who, with his contemporaries, has remained 'studiously ignorant of history, society, and human nature' (Peacock 2001: 693).

The harshness of this attack did not go unanswered, and Shelley's reply ends with the brilliant statement asserting the importance of the poet's role in society: 'Poets are the unacknowledged legislators of the world' (P. B. Shelley 1977: 508). Shelley was very clear that poets had a moral and political responsibility: he thought that poetry could effect change. Even the imagination in Shelley's *Defence* has a moral function:

> A man, to be greatly good, must imagine intensely and comprehensively; he must put himself in the place of another and of many others; the pains and pleasure of his species must become his own. The great instrument of moral good is the imagination. (P. B. Shelley 1977: 487–8)

The imagination, therefore, has a social function: it enables us to feel for one another and as one another. By empathizing with others, we can understand and move to reform the problems in contemporary society. Rather than feel that poetry should avoid or attempt to escape history, Shelley believed that the historical circumstance in which a poet lived determined his creation. In contrast to Peacock, he felt that their contemporaries 'surpass beyond comparison any who have appeared since the last national struggle for civil and religious liberty' (P. B. Shelley 1977: 508). Here, he is comparing Romantic poets to Milton and poets of that time who struggled for liberty from monarchical tyranny during the English Civil Wars of the seventeenth century. The 'electric life' which Shelley perceived was burning in the words of 'the most celebrated writers of the present day', is 'less their own spirit than the spirit of the age' (P. B. Shelley 1977: 508). In other words, poets are created by the historical times in which they live, they are a product of those times, and they singularly have the ability to influence and shape those times. 'Poets', he wrote in the Preface to *Prometheus Unbound*, 'are in one sense the creators, and in another the creations, of their age' (Wu 2006: 1094).

Victorian representations

In his prefaces to T. H. Ward's edition, *English Poets* (1880), and his own 1881 edition of Byron's poetry, the Victorian critic Matthew Arnold evaluated the Romantics, mentioning only Wordsworth, Coleridge, Byron, Shelley and Keats. These prefaces are interesting as we begin to see the Romantic canon being shaped and moulded. Male poets were not, in most cases, the most successful authors of the period, and it was during the Victorian period that they became particularly valued over female poets, novelists and playwrights. Women were neglected and ignored, creating a skewed sense of the texts produced and most appreciated during the period. Arnold's description of the five poets is also interesting. In particular, he describes Keats as 'having produced too little and being as yet too immature to rival' the others, and Shelley as a 'beautiful and ineffectual angel, beating in the void his luminous wings in vain' (Arnold 1964: 339–40). Arnold's comments on Shelley refuse to acknowledge the politics of his poetry and assign him to being a beautiful but ineffectual, other-worldly being, whilst Keats is regarded as the poet of unfulfilled promise. It is true that by the end of the Romantic period, usually signalled on university modules as sometime around 1837 (the year Queen Victoria came to the throne), many of these poets were dead and many had died young: Keats at 25, Shelley at 29 and Byron at 36. Their youth and early deaths were variously represented as evidence of their vulnerability and frailty.

From the moment of Keats's death, a degree of myth-making began, in Shelley's *Adonais* and other accounts of the poet's life and death. The painter Joseph Severn, who had been with Keats at his death, wrote to Keats's publisher, John Taylor, of his last days: 'that look was more than I could bear – the extreme brightness of his eyes – with his poor pallid face – was not earthly' (cited by Douglas-Fairhurst

2002: 9). This image of Keats was perpetuated through the remainder of the Romantic period and into the Victorian period, when the pervading myth was of his effeminacy, his delicacy, and the devastation caused by cruel treatment at the hands of the *Blackwood's* and *Quarterly* reviewers. Keats was transformed, much as Shelley was, into an effeminate and apolitical boy, who even in life was sickly and not long for this world. His poetry was considered escapism, a world of sensuousness and beauty that took him away from his physical and worldly sufferings. As Elizabeth Barrett-Browning put it: 'Keats was indeed a fine genius – too finely tuned for the gross dampness of our atmosphere [. . .] [H]e sang himself out of life' (cited by Douglas-Fairhurst 2002: 10). It took some time after his death for Keats's poetry to be republished (in 1829 there was a pirate edition published in Paris of the work of Shelley, Keats and Coleridge), but it caught the attention of Arthur Hallam and Tennyson and their circle, who also published the first English edition of *Adonais* in 1829 (Stillinger 2001: 250). In 1840 Keats's collected poems were reprinted and Richard Monckton Milnes' biography of the poet was published; from this point on 'Keats rapidly rose to canonicity' (Stillinger 2001: 246). Much of Shelley's political poetry did not see the light of day until many years after it had been written; when Mary Shelley published her 1824 edition of her husband's *Posthumous Poems*, it was quickly repressed by his father and many of the copies destroyed. It took until the formation of the Shelley Society in 1886 for many of his texts to be published and for *The Cenci* to be privately staged for the first time.

In 1847 the painter William Holman Hunt bought an edition of Keats's verse 'in book bins labelled "this lot 4d"' (cited in Wootton 1999: 160). The fact that Keats's book of poems was being sold for four pence tells us how his reputation had fared up to this point, and Arnold's dismissal of Keats reveals the way that many Victorians thought of him. Keats's poetry inspired Hunt to produce his first painting of a Keats subject, 'The Eve of St Agnes'; he told John Everett Millais of his 'discovery' of Keats, and when the painting was

hung in the Royal Academy, Dante Gabriel Rossetti came up
to Hunt 'repeating with emphasis his praise, and loudly
declaring that my picture [. . .] was the best in the collection'
(cited in Wootton 1999: 160). In 1848, the Pre-Raphaelite
Brotherhood was formed between Hunt, Millais and
Rossetti, and a love for Keats's poetry was an important part
of their work; scenes from Keats's poem 'La Belle Dame Sans
Merci' proved particularly inspirational to painters in the
mid- to late nineteenth and early twentieth centuries. Even
Keats's and Shelley's supporters contrived to represent a san-
itized version of their idols. George Bernard Shaw accused
the Shelley Society of a 'conspiracy' in trying 'to make
Shelley a saint' (cited by Steyaert 1991: 210). Shaw instead
emphasized Shelley's immense popularity among an audience of working men who had bought cheap, pirate editions
of his *Queen Mab*, which became known as the 'Chartist's
Bible'. Eventually Shelley would be reclaimed for the left,
once his political poetry had been revealed to the public.

Modernism and Romanticism

T. E. Hulme's lecture 'Romanticism and Classicism', which
was delivered in 1911 or 1912 but published posthumously
in 1924, argues that 'after a hundred years of romanticism,
we are in for a classical revival' (Hulme 1970: 55). Often,
Romanticism is defined by its difference to that which preceded it, in this case the classical, or more properly **neo-
classical** period of the eighteenth century. It is also possible,
as Hulme's essay proves, to define Romanticism in opposition
to a period that postdated it, the period of the early twentieth century that we would now call Modernism. In this
essay, Hulme reveals his distaste for Romanticism, which he
defines as influenced primarily by Rousseau's view of man.
Whereas, for the Romantics, 'man is intrinsically good, spoilt
by circumstance', for classicists, 'he is intrinsically limited,
but disciplined by order and tradition to something fairly
decent' (Hulme 1970: 57). Romanticism, according to
Hulme, considered man an 'infinite reservoir of possibilities';

in contrast, the classical view is that 'Man is an extraordinarily fixed and limited animal whose nature is absolutely constant. It is only by tradition and organisation that anything decent can be got out of him' (Hulme 1970: 57). Hulme famously described Romanticism as 'spilt religion' – religious feeling not channelled into its proper sphere. He argues that instead of believing in God or heaven, the Romantics believe in man as a god and a heaven on earth: 'It is like pouring a pot of treacle over the dinner table' (Hulme 1970: 58). The imagery he uses to describe Romantic poetry makes his opinion of it clear; he objects to its 'sloppiness'; that it is 'damp' (Hulme 1970: 61). Instead he wants a poem that is 'all dry and hard', one that is 'strictly confined to the earthly and the definite', and without Romanticism's 'vagueness': he admires poetry that is 'always perfectly human and never exaggerated: man is always a man and never a god' (Hulme 1970: 61–2). His prophecy 'that a period of dry, hard, classical verse is coming' was met in the early stages of Modernism, by the imagist poetry of which he was an early proponent (Hulme 1970: 63).

In 1939, feelings were such about the Romantics that C. S. Lewis would write of 'the modern dislike of the Romantics' (Lewis 1975: 324). He was writing this in answer to a specific attack by T. S. Eliot in a lecture delivered in 1933 on 'Shelley and Keats' (Eliot 1964). Eliot objected to Shelley and Shelley's poetry most virulently in this lecture on the grounds that he could not separate the man from the poetry and that he disliked the man intensely. This issue develops from ideas put forward in his essay of 1919, 'Tradition and the Individual Talent', where Eliot states that poetry is a 'process of depersonalisation': 'The progress of an artist [...] a continual extinction of personality' (Eliot 2001: 1094). In 'Shelley and Keats', he makes the point that it 'has become a commonplace to observe that Wordsworth's true greatness is independent of his opinions' (Eliot 1964: 87). While Wordsworth could be regarded in this way because, according to Eliot, his ideas and beliefs do not encroach upon the reader's enjoyment of his poetry, such an experience eludes

Eliot when reading Shelley. The problem is clearly not just the fact that Shelley intended his poetry to communicate his ideas, and that his poems have a political purpose, but also that Eliot disagrees with Shelley's politics. He refers to Shelley's youth throughout this and other criticism, but his is unlike Keats's, whose 'egotism, such as it is, is that of youth which time would have redeemed' (Eliot 1964: 100). Instead, Shelley's ideas are considered immature in the sense of 'childish or feeble' (Eliot 1964: 96). For Eliot, both Shelley's ideas and an enthusiasm for his poetry are products of 'adolescence' (Eliot 1964: 89). Ultimately, Eliot finds that he cannot 'ignore the "ideas" in Shelley's poems, so as to be able to enjoy the poetry', because those ideas can be 'so puerile that I cannot enjoy the poems in which they occur' (Eliot 1964: 90–1). C. S. Lewis makes the point that Shelley was disliked in the 1930s because his 'poetry is, to an unusual degree, entangled with political thought, and in a kind of political thought now generally unpopular' (Lewis 1975: 324). Eliot was politically conservative and found he could enjoy Keats because, unlike either Wordsworth or Shelley, 'he did not appear to have taken any absorbing interest in public affairs' (Eliot 1964: 102).

New criticism and beyond

Eliot refers in the lecture considered above to the work of I. A. Richards and to a further lack in Shelley's poetry of 'a precision of image and an economy' to which Richards had drawn attention (Eliot 1964: 90). Richards was a Cambridge literary critic, who first published his *Principles of Literary Criticism* in 1824; he used the method outlined in this book with his undergraduate students, removing names and dates from the literary texts in order to focus on interpretation. Another influential critic, F. R. Leavis, had a similar problem with Shelley's images, which, he wrote, have 'a general tendency [. . .] to forget the status of the metaphor or simile that introduced them and to assume an autonomy and a right to propagate' (Leavis 1936: 206). Any insistence that the historical and social circumstances of literature had no bearing on a text's meaning did not bode well for some of the Romantics, particularly those who did not divorce their political beliefs from their poetical objectives. In 1953, M. H. Abrams published one of the most influential accounts of Romanticism, returning it to the centre of critical appreciation in *The Mirror and the Lamp*. In this book, Abrams presented a diagram which showed how the 'work' connected with the 'universe', 'artist' and 'audience' (Abrams 1953: 6). He argued that, previous to the Romantic period, literature had been more concerned with the relationship between the work and the universe, privileging mimetic art that best imitated the world it described. With the Romantic period came a greater emphasis on the relationship between the work and the artist, with the work instead regarded as expressive of the artist's vision (Abrams 1953: 3). Abrams opens *The Mirror and the Lamp* with the statement that modern literary theory began in the Romantic period and describes how different theories have privileged specific elements and relationships between these four elements: work, artist, audience and universe (Abrams 1953: vii, 6–7).

Abrams taught another important Romantic critic, Harold Bloom, at Cornell University, who also helped to rescue the reputation of the Romantics when they were not especially popular. Bloom also cited as a major influence the critic Northrop Frye, who had been instrumental in bringing Blake into the Romantic canon. Frye thought of literary criticism as a kind of science, and a discipline in its own right. He developed what he called 'archetypal or myth criticism' in his book *Anatomy of Criticism* (1957), which challenged the dominance of the New Critical method. Rather than pursue the 'close reading' of texts, Frye argued that one needed to 'stand back from the poem' in order to see its 'archetypal organization' (cited in Leitch 2001: 1442). The ideas contained in this book had begun with his first book *Fearful Symmetry* (1947), which had concentrated on the symbolism used by Blake. In his later book *Anatomy of Criticism*, he extended this argument to consider the importance that symbols used in literature had for our interpretation of it. The psychologist Carl Jung has been seen as one of Frye's major sources and psychoanalysis was also important in the formation of Harold Bloom's most famous contribution to literary theory, his book *The Anxiety of Influence* (1975). Blake is in many ways the most important Romantic for Bloom because in his writings he finds someone who 'strives to replace nature with art and previous poems with his own work' (Lietch 2001: 1795). In *The Anxiety of Influence* he describes how Romantic poets are engaged in an Oedipal struggle with their literary forebears 'even to the death' in an attempt to find their own voice (Bloom 2001: 1797).

CURRENT ISSUES AND DEBATES

This section considers the main critical schools to have affected the study of Romanticism since the work of Abrams, Bloom and Frye, considering deconstruction and the work of Geoffrey Hartman first. Since the 1980s, important New Historicist criticism has considered Romantic writings within their historical and political moment. Much work has been done to redress the balance in favour of writers overlooked by such critics; the study of women writers, in particular, has made it clear that female authors were among the most popular and most influential in their day.

Deconstruction

The theory known as deconstruction has also been influential as a way of thinking about Romantic texts. Deconstruction is a critical approach that emerged in the 1960s influenced by Jacques Derrida, which subverts or undermines the operation of assigning meaning to language. Instead the referent is recognized as being always deferred and that therefore we can never get beyond language. The writings of Wordsworth and Percy Shelley have been particularly fruitful for the deconstructive critics Geoffrey Hartman and Paul de Man. For instance, Hartman finds in Wordsworth's poetry a path 'through a depression clearly linked to the ravage of self-consciousness and the "strong disease" of self-analysis' (Hartman 1993: 43). Hartman's background was in New Criticism, but he became influenced by deconstruction, and his 'own brand of mildly speculative and densely textual criticism' can be seen as 'an attempt at reconciliation' between textual and philosophic approaches (Selden, Widdowson and Brooker 1997: 182). Christopher Norris describes how Hartman had 'begun to fret under the various constraints of the New Critical method. Deconstruction offered the enticing prospect of a criticism free to explore whatever stylistic possibilities it chose, without observing any strict demarcation between "creative" and (merely) "critical" writing' (Norris 2002: 91). Similarly, Paul de Man used the Romantics to develop his deconstructionist theories, 'indeed, de Man argues that the Romantics actually deconstruct their own writing' (Selden, Widdowson and Brooker 1997: 176). Certain Romantic writers seem peculiarly aware of language's sceptical relationship to meaning; language is recognized as doomed to fail, unable to represent the referent: 'a voice / Is wanting', as Shelley said; 'the deep truth is imageless' (*Prometheus Unbound*, Wu 2006: 1131). In Wordsworth's case, the perceived distinction between 'spots of time' (discussed in the previous section) and the moment of his composition mean that he is always attempting to return to his boyhood through memory but is simultaneously acutely aware that he will fail in his attempt. Indeed, the recognition in 'Tintern Abbey' that he is now 'changed, no doubt, from what I was when first / I came among these hills' leads Wordsworth to reveal that he cannot return to the unmediated passion of his youth: 'I cannot paint / What then I was' (Wu 2006: 409).

New Historicism

One of the most influential critical approaches for the Romantic period has been that of New Historicism, which appears to have been especially suggestive to critics of the Renaissance and the Romantic periods of literature. Emerging in opposition to New Criticism and deconstruction, New Historicism reads a text in its historical context with an understanding that texts engage with and influence that history. Accepting post-structuralist views of language and ideology, New Historicist critics find that texts reflect, reproduce or challenge the dominant discourse of the Romantic period. This approach is typified in Britain by Marilyn Butler's 1981 book *Romantics, Rebels and Reactionaries* and in North America by Jerome McGann's *The Romantic Ideology* (1983). Central to this approach is a consideration of the relationship between literature and the historical circumstances of its composition. The subtitle to Butler's book is *English Literature and its Background, 1760–1830* and it is the relationship between 'literature' and 'background' that is further explored by these critics.

This guide to Romanticism has itself been organized around the idea that these two things are different and can be kept separate: Chapter 1 deals with the historical, cultural and intellectual context of the literature that is discussed in Chapter 2. This structure suggests that the meaning of a text can be further explicated by revealing the context in which it was written. In fact, this is not the only context available. Besides the moment of the text's composition, there is also that of its publication and its reception. Furthermore, much has happened between that time and this. What is the context of a Romantic-period reading of the text, and what is the relationship between then and now? The first section of Chapter 3 gave some indication of Romanticism's critical fortunes during the intervening period, considering how it came to be identified, how definitions changed over time, and how it has meant different things to different critics because of both their historical period and their critical approach. It is, of course, ultimately impossible to fully recreate the historical moments of a text's composition, publication or reception. Marilyn Butler notes that 'Romanticism, in the full sense in which we now know it, is a posthumous movement; something different was experienced at the time' (Butler 1981: 2).

Butler argues that 'culture is a way of expressing experience', in other words, that literature should be regarded as part of culture, reacting to and reflecting as much as creating society's ideologies (Butler 1981: 4). In this, she can be seen as reacting to Abrams as much as to New Critical tendencies, since Abrams' diagram discussed in the last section suggested a simple relationship between, and autonomy of, the 'universe' and the 'work' (Abrams 1953). In fact, Butler is claiming that neither the work nor the author should be thought of in isolation, nor should the relationship between the two be considered a 'closed system' (Butler 1981: 9). Butler argues that rather than think of a book as the product of one man,

> [a] book is made by its public, the readers it literally finds and the people in the author's mind's eye. Literature, like all art, like language, is a collective activity, powerfully conditioned by social forces, what needs to be and may be said in a particular community at a given time [. . .] authors are not the solitaries of the Romantic myth, but citizens. Within any community tastes, opinions, values, the shaping stuff of art, are socially generated. (Butler 1981: 10)

Current historicist criticism is new because it is alive to many of the problems that have limited historical studies of literature previously. It is clear that structuralist and post-structuralist ideas of language and identity have changed the way that critics now regard their sense of history. Instead of considering history to be true fact, they are aware of the narratives that histories spin; the issue of giving cultural value to literary texts, the fact that meaning in texts needs to be 'disentangled' rather than 'deciphered'; and that, as Roland Barthes argued, a text is 'a tissue of quotations drawn from the innumerable centres of culture' (Barthes 2001: 1468).

Historicists have been criticized for being unaware of, or trying to hide, the fact that in returning to the past they may have specific ideological points they wish to prove. They may, in fact, be looking for something and be creating that past, rather than objectively regarding *Things As They Are* (to borrow Godwin's extended title for *Caleb Williams*). The past which is unearthed in research may owe more to present interests than to the concerns of contemporary writers. Critics may, for example, have privileged the Romantics' liberal attitudes, such as their campaigns against slavery, because that is what they wanted to find in them. McGann's *Romantic Ideology* (1983) criticized Romanticists for being insufficiently critical of the terms Romantics themselves used; they had been taken in by 'an uncritical absorption in Romanticism's own self-representations' (McGann 1983: 1). They are seen to purvey a certain myth in their work, of which the self-conscious critic needs to be aware.

> The poetry of Romanticism is everywhere marked by extreme forms of displacement and poetic conceptualization whereby the actual human issues with which the poetry is concerned are resituated in a variety of idealized localities. A socio-historical method pursued within the Critical tradition helps to expose these dramas of displacement and idealization without, at the same time, debunking or deconstructing the actual works themselves. (McGann 1981: 1)

Wordsworth, in particular, has been seen as deliberately turning away from explicit political or social comment to hide in 'Romanticism's own self-representations'; the very fact that he does not refer explicitly to socio-political issues of his day in his poems is seen as evidence of his concern with these issues. Kenneth R. Johnston describes this position in the poem 'Tintern Abbey': 'Wordsworth's "oversight" [. . .] of the busy charcoal industry around Tintern thus could be, through its very oblique presence in the poem [. . .] a kind of hint that he wishes to ignore the economical industrial realities of his time and place' (Johnston 2005: 170).

Recently, critics have countered the arguments of New Historicists such as McGann, Marjorie Levinson and David Simpson by claiming that instead of displacing politics, the Romantics make specific and explicit contributions to contemporary debates. Tim Fulford considers Wordsworth's neglected late poem 'The Haunted Tree', 'an intelligent and witty, if oblique, contribution to contemporary political and social debate' rather than 'a flight from political issues into the sublime area of his own subjectivity' (Fulford 2001: 34). Instead of finding John Thelwall's essays a 'pastoral retreat from social strife', Michael Scrivener argues that the texts are 'marked everywhere by political hope and anxiety' (Scrivener 2001: 73). In a similar move, Nicholas Roe has countered Levinson's sense of Keats's 'social and cultural removal', instead ascribing genuinely 'dissenting motives' to his literary ambitions (Roe 1997: 14–15). Keats, particularly, is someone who has benefited from recent historical investigation: critics have tried to put right 'the idea that he lived in a vacuum, and never described or responded to wider issues' (Motion 1997: xxii). James Chandler, in *England in 1819*, has argued persuasively that the Romantic period was, as he puts it, 'The Age of the Spirit of the Age' (Chandler 1998: 105). In this book, he states that the Romantics themselves were historicist; in other words, that Romantic writers were aware that they must 'creat[e] the *history* by which they must be understood' (Johnston 2005: 167).

Much of the current work that has been done more recently in Romanticism has been based on a new conception of a text's relationship to its context. Some areas of research can be grouped under the title 'recovery research', attempting to recover the original social and historical culture of Romantic texts. This kind of work has pointed out that our Romantic canon of the 'big six' is a product of Victorian critics rather than of the Romantic period itself, and has sought to retrieve the writings of marginalized groups and bring them to the foreground, such as women, black writers, labouring-class writers, and lesbian and gay writers. Returning to a sense of the actual culture of the time reveals, for instance, that there were not the divisions then that we place on disciplines today. There were not 'two cultures' of arts and sciences, for example, and many writers such as Percy Shelley and Joseph Priestley would have denied the limitations placed upon them by such divisions. Historicist critical work also denies an idea of Romanticism as the product of a solitary 'genius', instead seeing it as produced by social, historical and political forces.

Women Romantic writers

Some of the most impressive recent critical work done on the Romantic period has revealed that the canon has skewed our knowledge of the importance of women's writing. As Stuart Curran put it in his highly influential essay, 'Romantic Poetry: The I Altered': 'Manifest distortions of the record have accrued' (Curran 1996: 279). Curran uses a list of 39 female poets, novelists and playwrights put together by the Romantic poet, Mary Robinson, to argue that:

> the breadth of the list should remind us from the start that by the 1790s in Great Britain there were many more women than men novelists and that the theatre was actually dominated by women, all the more when Joanna Baillie's fame and influence spread. In the arena of poetry [. . .] the place of women was likewise, at least for a time, predominant, and it is here that the distortions of our received history are most glaring. Its chronology has been written wholly, and arbitrarily, along a masculine gender line. (Curran 1996: 280)

In fact, as Paula Feldman and Teresa M. Kelley have pointed out, Felicia Hemans was the bestselling writer of the Romantic period; her work 'was admired by Byron, Shelley, Wordsworth, Matthew Arnold, William Michael Rossetti, George Eliot, Elizabeth Barrett' (Feldman and Kelley 1995: 2). Walter Scott called Joanna Baillie ' "the best dramatic writer" in Britain "since the days of Shakespeare and Massinger" ' (Feldman and Kelley 1995: 4). Furthermore, Wordsworth's Preface to the *Lyrical Ballads* 'appropriated without acknowledgement' Baillie's plea for a more natural language to be used in literature (Feldman and Kelley 1995: 5). Coleridge used the sonnets of Charlotte

Smith to learn how to write them himself (Feldman and Kelley 1995: 5). Curran singles out the literary achievements of Anna Barbauld 'with five editions of her poems between 1773 and 1777'; Hannah More 'with six sizable volumes of verse between 1773 and 1786'; Charlotte Smith 'whose *Elegiac Sonnets* went through ten expanding editions in fifteen years'; and Helen Maria Williams who published her collected *Poems, in Two Volumes* aged only 24 (Curran 1996: 281).

Anne Mellor writes that once we 'focus our attention on the numerous women writers who produced at least half of the literature published in England between 1780 and 1830', we gain a new and radically different understanding of Romanticism (Mellor 1993: 1). Women writers, Mellor argues, write about different things in different ways; indeed, she considers that there is a 'masculine' and a 'feminine' Romanticism:

> . . . even a cursory, introductory survey reveals significant differences between the thematic concerns, formal practices, and ideological positionings of male and female Romantic writers. To mention only the most immediately obvious, the women writers of the Romantic period for the most part forswore the concern of their male peers with the capacities of the creative imagination, with the limitations of language, with the possibility of transcendence or 'unity of being,' with the development of an autonomous self, with political (as opposed to social) revolution, with the role of the creative writer as political leader or religious saviour. Instead, women Romantic writers tended to celebrate, not the achievements of the imagination nor the overflow of powerful feelings, but rather the workings of the rational mind, a mind relocated – in a gesture of revolutionary gender implications – in the female as well as the male body. They thus insisted upon the fundamental equality of women and men. (Mellor 1993: 2–3)

Mellor here highlights the various types of 'Romanticism' available at the time, a multivalency that had been hidden by studies simply based on the canonical male poets. Recent criticism has not only considered the existence of women writers in the period, and how recognizing their success alters the landscape of Romanticism, but it has also raised an issue over the way that women were represented by male writers. Vivien Jones has investigated how female-conduct books, Burke's aesthetic theories of **the sublime and the beautiful**, and contemporary accounts of women writers as 'unsexed', reveal that ' "woman" was a culturally defined category which women had to negotiate and to suffer' (Jones 1990: 6).

Romanticism and post-colonialism

Historicist research has also highlighted certain other areas of Romantic culture, including the impact that Britain's growing Empire had on the literature produced at the time. Deirdre Coleman points out that 'by 1820 Britain ruled 200 million people, over a quarter of the world's population', and that it was difficult to find anyone not involved in some way or another with the 'imperial system' (Coleman 2005: 237). From the 1770s onwards, the anti-slavery movement began drawing attention to the slave trade, often using literature and the arts to argue its case. The writings of former slaves are also the subject of post-colonial investigation into the Romantic period. The African, Phillis Wheatley, who had been captured and brought to America, for example, was forced to publish her *Poems on Various Subjects* in London in 1773 because publishers in Boston had refused to. Though Wheatley's poetry largely concerned religious and moral subjects, other Africans wrote books that aided the abolitionist movement, such as that by Olaudah Equiano, *The Interesting Narrative of the Life of Olaudah Equiano, or Gustavus Vassa the African* (1789). Equiano, who had bought his freedom in 1766 for £40, was something of a celebrity in England after the publication of his autobiography, which was immensely successful and influential. These authors' marginalized voices provide a dissident perspective to that of the dominant white European. Critics have considered the representations of 'othered' peoples in literature of the Romantic period, particularly in writings concerned with the 'East', an unspecified region set up in opposition to an equally unspecified 'West'. This kind of writing – making the exotic into an alien 'other' – is the practice of Orientalism as defined by Edward Said (Said 1978). The role of science in communicating racist ideology has also recently come under scrutiny, as has the intersection between travel and science in the colonial world. The methods of post-colonialism have also proved fruitful in opening up discussions of other marginalized voices, such as those of the labouring-class writers considered in the previous chapter. Indeed, using a method of cultural history rather than giving attention solely to the literary text has shown the symbiotic relationship that exists between many different disciplines and literature; and the text itself can be considered as a reflection of Romantic society's fears, hopes and fantasies.

4

Resources for Independent Study

Chronology
Glossary of Key Literary Terms and Concepts
Further Reading and Resources

CHRONOLOGY

1773 Anna Laetitia Aikin (married name Barbauld), *Poems*; and with John Aikin, *Miscellaneous Pieces in Prose*

1775 American War of Independence begins

1776 American Declaration of Independence

1777 Richard Brinsley Sheridan's *School for Scandal* first performed at Drury Lane Theatre in London

1778 Fanny Burney, *Evelina*

1780 Gordon Riots in London

1783 William Pitt, the Younger, becomes prime minister

1783 Mongolfier brothers give the first public demonstration of their hot-air balloon

1784 Charlotte Smith, *Elegiac Sonnets*

1785 Ann Yearsley, *Poems, on Several Occasions*

1785 William Cowper, *The Task*; William Beckford, *Vathek*

1787 Impeachment of Warren Hastings

1787 Committee for the Abolition of the Slave-Trade formed

1788 Hannah More, *Slavery: A Poem*; Yearsley, *Poem on the Inhumanity of the Slave Trade*

1789 (14 July) Storming of the Bastille in France

1789   (August) *Declaration of the Rights of Man and of the Citizen*
approved by the National Assembly in France

1790   Edmund Burke, *Reflections on the Revolution in France*;
Mary Wollstonecraft, *Vindication of the Rights of Men*;
Joanna Baillie, *Poems*; William Blake, *The Marriage of
Heaven and Hell*; Ann Radcliffe, *A Sicilian Romance*;
Helen Maria Williams, *Letters Written in France*

1791   Birmingham riots in which Joseph Priestley's house
and laboratory are destroyed; (June) Slave rebellion
in St Domingue (Haiti); Thomas Paine, *Rights of
Man* (Part One); Anna Barbauld, *Epistle to William
Wilberforce*; *An Address to the Opposers of the Repeal of the
Test and Corporation Acts*; Erasmus Darwin, *The Botanic
Garden*; Elizabeth Inchbald, *A Simple Story*; Hannah
More, *Cheap Repository Tracts*; Mary Robinson, *Poems*

1792   'September Massacres' in Paris; (April) France
declares war on Austria and Prussia; London
Corresponding Society established; Paine charged
with sedition and sentenced to death; Mary
Wollstonecraft, *Vindication of the Rights of Woman*; Anna
Barbauld, *Civic Sermons to the People*; William Gilpin,
Essays on Picturesque Beauty

1793   (21 January) King Louis XVI executed in France;
(February) England declares war on France;
(September) the 'Terror' begins; (October) French
Girondins executed; William Godwin, *Enquiry into
Political Justice*; Blake, *Visions of the Daughters of Albion*;
Charlotte Smith, *The Old Manor House*

1794   (May) Habeas Corpus suspended; (July) Robespierre
arrested and guillotined; (November) Treason Trials
in which Thomas Holcroft, John Thelwall and Horne
Tooke are tried and acquitted; Blake, *Europe, Songs of
Innocence and of Experience* and *Urizen*; Godwin, *Caleb
Williams, or, Things As They Are*; Radcliffe, *The Mysteries
of Udolpho*

1795   'Two Acts', otherwise known as the 'Gagging Acts'
passed: the Seditious Meetings Act and the
Treasonable Practices Act; stones thrown at George

III's carriage at the opening of Parliament; Maria Edgeworth, *Letters for Literary Ladies*

1796 French invasion threat; Edward Jenner performs first smallpox vaccination; William Beckford begins building Fonthill Abbey; Samuel Taylor Coleridge, *Poems on Various Subjects*; Matthew Lewis, *The Monk*; Robinson, *Sappho and Phaon*; Anna Seward, *Llangollen Vale, with Other Poems*; Ann Yearsley, *The Rural Lyre*

1797 Peace treaty agreed between France and Austria; republican governments declared in Venice, Genoa and Milan; naval mutinies at Spithead and Nore are suppressed; painter J. M. W. Turner tours the Lake District; the *Anti-Jacobin* first published; Radcliffe, *The Italian*

1798 Rebellion in Ireland suppressed; Napoleon invades Egypt; Battle of the Nile, in which Nelson defeats French forces; alliance formed between Britain, Austria, Naples, Portugal, Russia, Turkey; income tax introduced in Britain; Thomas Malthus, *Essay on the Principle of Population*; William Wordsworth and S. T. Coleridge, *Lyrical Ballads*; Joanna Baillie, *A Series of Plays: In Which it is Attempted to Delineate the Stronger Passions of the Mind [. . .]*; Godwin, *Memoirs of the Author of a Vindication of the Rights of Woman*; Wordsworth finishes the first two-book version of *The Prelude* (not published until 1850)

1799 Combination Laws passed to suppress trade unions; Napoleon becomes First Consul in France; Rosetta Stone discovered in Egypt; Lewis, *Tales of Terror*; Seward, *Original Sonnets*

1800 (February) Act of Union with Ireland; Malta surrenders to the British; Alessandro Volta invents the electrical battery; Robinson, *Lyrical Tales*

1801 George III refuses to pass bill allowing Catholic emancipation; Pitt resigns; Henry Addington, later Lord Sidmouth, becomes prime minister in Britain (until 1804); Union Jack becomes the British flag; Thomas Jefferson is elected President of America;

Toussaint L'Ouverture liberates black slaves in St Domingo; Robert Southey, *Thalaba, the Destroyer*; James Hogg, *Scottish Pastorals, Poems and Songs*

1802   (March) The Peace of Amiens is negotiated between Britain and France, which lasts for 14 months; Health and Morals of Apprentices Act fixed a 12-hour working day for children and other regulations for the health and safety of 'pauper apprentices'; *Edinburgh Review* first published, under the editorship of Francis Jeffrey; The *Weekly Political Register* first published by William Cobbett; Thomas Chatterton, *Collected Works*

1803   (April) The United States purchases Louisiana from France; (May) war is again declared against France; execution of Robert Emmet (he is hanged, drawn and quartered) after the failed Irish rebellion; Toussaint L'Ouverture dies of pneumonia in a French prison; Erasmus Darwin, *The Temple of Nature*

1804   Pitt forms his second coalition government; Napoleon becomes Emperor of France

1805   (October) Battle of Trafalgar; Walter Scott, *The Lay of the Last Minstrel*; Godwin, *Fleetwood; or, The New Man of Feeling*

1806   Lord William Grenville becomes prime minister; Constable tours the Lake District; Robinson, *Poetical Works*

1807   Grenville resigns over issue of Catholic emancipation; William Bentinck, Duke of Portland, becomes prime minister; (25 March) Abolition of the Slave Trade Bill passed; beginning of the Peninsular War; Charles and Mary Lamb publish *Tales from Shakespeare*; Charlotte Smith, *Beachy Head and Other Poems* published post-humously; Wordsworth *Poems, in Two Volumes*

1808   (August) Convention of Cintra agreed between Britain and France; John Dalton, *New System of Chemical Philosophy* (Part One); Hemans, *England and Spain; or, Valour and Patriotism*; Scott, *Marmion*; the newspaper *The Liberal* is first published, edited by Leigh Hunt

1809   Portland resigns; Spencer Percival becomes prime minister; Napoleon is excommunicated after challenging the power of the papacy; the *Quarterly Review* first published, under the editorship of William Gifford; gas-lighting used in central London for the first time; Byron, *English Bards and Scotch Reviewers*; Coleridge first publishes the journal *The Friend* (runs until 1810); Charles and Mary Lamb publish *Poetry for Children*

1810   King George III is officially declared 'insane'; Joanna Baillie, *The Family Legend*; Scott, *The Lady of the Lake*; Seward, *Poetical Works*; Southey, *The Curse of Kehema*

1811   (5 February) Prince of Wales becomes Prince Regent; (November) Luddite disturbances begin in the Midlands; Jane Austen, *Sense and Sensibility*; Percy Shelley and Thomas Jefferson Hogg publish *The Necessity of Atheism* and are expelled from University College, Oxford

1812   (11 May) Percival assassinated in the House of Commons; Robert Jenkinson, Lord Liverpool becomes prime minister; Lord Castlereagh becomes foreign secretary and Lord Sidmouth the home secretary; Toleration Act passed permitting greater freedom for Protestant Non-Conformists; (June) Napoleon invades Russia but retreats from Moscow later this year; Byron's maiden speech in the House of Lords in support of the Luddites and Catholic emancipation; cantos I and II of George Gordon Byron's *Childe Harold's Pilgrimage* published; Barbauld, *Eighteen Hundred and Eleven*; George Crabbe, *Tales* (referred to in Austen's *Mansfield Park*); Felicia Hemans, *Domestic Affections, and Other Poems*

1813   Luddite leaders tried at York, 17 men are executed and many others transported; Hunt imprisoned for libelling the Prince Regent; Southey becomes Poet Laureate after Walter Scott refuses; Austen, *Pride and Prejudice*; Byron, *The Giaour* and *The Bride of Abydos*; Percy Shelley, *Queen Mab*; Coleridge's play *Remorse* published and performed at Drury Lane Theatre in London; Scott, *Rokeby, A Poem*

1814   (March) Paris falls to allies; Napoleon abdicates and is exiled to the island Elba; the Bourbon monarchy is restored in France and Europe redrawn at the Congress of Vienna; Austen, *Mansfield Park*; Byron, *Corsair* and *Lara*; Scott, *Waverley*; Hunt, *Feast of the Poets*; Wordsworth, *The Excursion*

1815   Napoleon escapes from Elba and returns to rule for the 'Hundred Days'; (18 June) Battle of Waterloo; allied armies defeat the French; (15 July) Napoleon surrenders and is exiled to St Helena; Louis XVIII restored to the French throne; Corn Laws passed to protect the price of wheat for British landowners, preventing the importation of grain from outside the UK before it reached a certain price; John Nash starts to rebuild Brighton Pavillion for the Prince Regent; Byron, *Hebrew Melodies*; Scott, *Guy Mannering*; Wordsworth, *Poems* and *The White Doe of Rylstone*

1816   (December) Spa Fields Riot in Britain; Austen, *Emma*; Byron publishes the third canto of *Childe Harold's Pilgrimage* and *The Prisoner of Chillon*; Coleridge, *Christabel, Kubla Khan* and *The Pains of Sleep*; Scott, *The Antiquary*; Hunt, *The Story of Rimini*; Percy Shelley, *Alastor [. . .] and Other Poems*

1817   (March) Habeas Corpus suspended; Elgin Marbles purchased for the British Museum by the British Government; Byron, *Manfred: A Dramatic Poem*; Cobbett, *English Grammar*; Godwin, *Mandeville*; *Blackwood's Edinburgh Magazine* first published; Coleridge, *Biographia Literaria* and *Sibylline Leaves*; Keats, *Poems*; William Hazlitt, *Characters of Shakespeare's Plays* and *The Round Table*; Hemans, *Modern Greece*; Thomas Moore, *Lalla Rookh*

1818   Francis Burdett's Bill for reform (including universal male suffrage) is defeated in Parliament; Austen's *Northanger Abbey* and *Persuasion* published posthumously; Keats, *Endymion*; Mary Shelley, *Frankenstein, or,* *the Modern Prometheus*, Hazlitt, *Lectures on the English Poets*; Hunt, *Foliage*

1819 Passing of the 'six acts': the Training Prevention Act; the Seizure of Arms Act; the Seditious Meetings Prevention Act; the Blasphemous and Seditious Libels Act; the Misdemeanours Act; the Newspaper and Stamp Duties Act; (16 August) Peterloo Massacre; Byron, cantos I and II of *Don Juan*; Shelley, *Rosalind and Helen [. . .] with Other Poems* and *The Cenci*; Crabbe, *Tales of the Hall*; Hemans, *Tales and Historic Scenes in Verse*; Scott, *Ivanhoe*; Wordsworth, *Peter Bell*

1820 (January) Revolution in Spain; (July) Revolution in Naples; King George III dies; Prince Regent becomes King George IV; Cato Street Conspiracy to kill several government ministers fails and the leaders are executed; the Queen Caroline affair; the Bill of Pains and Penalties, which would have deprived Caroline of the title of Queen and divorced her from George IV, is withdrawn from Parliament; *London Magazine* first published; Royal Astronomical Society founded; Clare, *Poems, Descriptive of Rural Life and Scenery*; Keats, *Lamia, Isabella, The Eve of St Agnes and Other Poems*; Percy Shelley, *The Cenci, Prometheus Unbound [. . .] with Other Poems*

1821 Greek War of Independence begins; Byron, *Marino Faliero, Sardanapalus, The Two Foscari, Cain*, cantos III–V of *Don Juan*; Clare, *The Village Minstrel*; Thomas De Quincey, *Confessions of an Opium Eater*; Percy Shelley, *Adonais* and *Epipsychidion*; Hazlitt begins publishing the magazine *Table Talk*

1822 Hemans, *Welsh Melodies*; Scott, *The Fortunes of Nigel*

1823 Byron, cantos VI–XIV of *Don Juan*; Charles Lamb publishes the first series of *Essays of Elia*; Hemans, *The Siege of Valencia, and Other Poems*; *The Lancet* first published

1824 Combinations Act repealed (see 1799); Royal Society for the Prevention of Cruelty to Animals founded; National Gallery in London opens; Byron, cantos

XV–XVI of *Don Juan* published posthumously; Hogg, *Confessions of a Justified Sinner*; Landon, *The Improvisatrice*; Scott, *Redgauntlet*; Mary Shelley edits and publishes Percy Shelley's *Posthumous Poems*

1825 First steam locomotive railway opens; Barbauld, *Works* published posthumously; Hazlitt, *The Spirit of the Age*; Coleridge, *Aids to Reflection*

1826 University College, London, founded; Mary Shelley, *The Last Man*; Hazlitt, *The Plain Speaker*

1827 Clare, *The Shepherd's Calendar*

GLOSSARY OF KEY LITERARY TERMS AND CONCEPTS

Ballad

A poetic genre that usually takes the form of quatrains (four-line stanzas), with the second and fourth lines rhyming. The first and third lines often have four stresses per line and the second and fourth three stresses per line. Traditionally this was a form associated with folk-songs that were transmitted orally over the generations; Wordsworth's and Coleridge's *Lyrical Ballads* radically redefined the form, creating what we would now call the literary ballad.

Bluestockings

A loosely defined group of largely female writers collected around Elizabeth Montagu. They consisted of two generations of poets, novelists and educationalists, with the first generation supporting the work of the younger ones. Women associated with the Bluestockings included Frances Boscawen, Elizabeth Carter, Hester Thrale Piozzi, Hannah More, Fanny Burney, Anna Barbauld and Ann Yearsley. The term 'Bluestocking' was also used by male writers to deprecate the intellectual achievements of these women.

Closet drama

A genre of dramatic writing. Examples include Byron's *Manfred* (a 'Dramatic Poem') and Percy Shelley's *Prometheus*

Unbound (a 'lyrical drama'). These texts are written in the form of a play but were never meant to be performed; rather they were written to be read either alone or aloud within a group or **coterie**. This allowed the author to include scenes that would be difficult to stage or that they could not trust a manager to produce well. It also allowed for subject matter that was too risqué for theatre, such as the incest suggested in *Manfred*.

Coterie
A group of like-minded individuals who share political goals and seek to achieve these goals through their writings. They tend to be avant-garde, or have ideals that are in some way ahead of their times, and try to live their lives according to their principles. The literature produced by a coterie member is often read in manuscript form by other members who might comment on it, correct it, respond creatively themselves, or see it through publication on their behalf, creating a sense of dialogue between coterie members.

Dissenter (incl. Unitarian)
Those who dissented to, and had separated from, the established churches of England and Wales. Some dissenters were granted the right to worship as Non-Conformists by the Act of Toleration of 1688, but this did not apply to Unitarians. Certain specific rights were withheld for all Dissenters, such as the right to hold public office or attend university, until the repeal of the Test and Corporations Act in 1828.

Enlightenment
Also known as the Age of Reason, this term refers to the historical period and cultural movement that preceded Romanticism. There was a sense that the 'dark ages' of superstition, barbarity, ignorance and prejudice were being replaced by reason and progress. The ideals of the Enlightenment can be found in both the American and the French Revolutions.

Girondins

The Girondins or Girondists were a political faction within the National Convention during the France Revolution, many of whom came from the Gironde region in France, and who gathered in the salon of a political activist, Marie Roland, in the early 1790s. They were more radical in their views than other political groups at the time, and were against the idea of monarchy and instead wanted France to be a democratic republic. These figures influenced certain writers labelled '**Jacobins**' in Britain, including William Godwin, Mary Wollstonecraft, Helen Maria Williams and Thomas Holcroft. They were early victims of the Terror, many of their deputies being guillotined in October 1793.

Gothic

A revival in Gothic architecture and art of the medieval period preceded the rise of Gothicism in literature, which rejected the reason and enlightenment of the **Neo-Classical** period. Gothic novels and poems were set in medieval castles, dungeons, crumbling towers and monasteries, with a narrative often involving the supernatural and the oppression or tyrannizing of an innocent heroine. The object was to produce a pleasurable horror in the reader, which can be linked with the experience of the **sublime**.

Romantic Hellenism

Refers to the sympathy which Romantic writers held for the ancient Greeks, and which had particular topicality after the Greeks' bid for independence and subsequent war with the Turks. There was a renewed interest in Greek art when Greece became a popular destination on the grand tour, and with the purchase of important artefacts such as the 'Elgin Marbles', so called because Lord Elgin brought them to Britain from the Parthenon. Percy Shelley wrote: 'We are all Greeks – our laws, our literature, our religion, our arts have their root in Greece' (Preface to *Hellas*, 1821, P. B. Shelley 1977: 409).

Industrialization

The Industrial Revolution began in the Romantic period, accompanied by great advances in industry and technology and increased urbanization. The negative effects of such advances can be witnessed in Blake's poems, such as 'London' in *The Songs of Experience*, where there are references to child labour, prostitution and the urbanization of populations. The Luddite disturbances in Britain throughout this period can also be associated with the effects of industrialization; men accused of machine-breaking were punished harshly, often being transported or executed.

Jacobin (and Anti-Jacobin)

The Jacobins of the French Revolution were members of a society called the Jacobin Club, but in Britain this term was used more freely to mean anyone with radical political views. The polarization of political opinion in the period led to the label being defined by its opposition; the *Anti-Jacobin* was a magazine set up by the Tory minister George Canning, which targeted British writers who supported the French Revolution.

Jacobite and Jacobitism

Jacobites wished for the return of the Stuart kings to the throne, after they were deposed by William and Mary in the so-called 'Glorious Revolution' of 1688. (Their name comes from King James II who had been deposed.) This group therefore supported the Jacobite risings of 1715 and 1745. Walter Scott uses the backdrop of these risings in his novels *Waverley* and *The Bride of Lammermoor*.

Laissez-Faire (free trade)

Replacing a system called mercantilism as the dominant economic theory, and continuing to this day, free-trade economics does not restrict or hinder the flow of goods or ervices by means of tariffs or protectionist policies. Adam Smith, in the *Wealth of Nations*, was an early proponent of free trade. In the Romantic period, protectionist policies included the Corn Laws, a tax on corn imported into Britain, introduced in 1815 and repealed in 1845.

Millenarianism
A belief in an apocalypse, after which there will be a thousand-year period of peace on earth and then an eternity in heaven. The cataclysmic event of the French Revolution suggested the coming of the millennium to many. Robert Southey wrote: 'Old things seemed passing away, and nothing was dreamt of but the regeneration of the human race' (cited in Norton 2000, vol. 2: 15).

Nationalism
During the Romantic period many nations were formed, as many wars were fought for political independence and others sought to promote an idea of a coherent national identity. A nation might be imagined as such because of a shared language, culture and religion; national identity can be promoted through symbols, anthems, other music and the arts. Nations in the Romantic period, such as France and England, defined themselves in opposition to each other according to their ideological differences.

Neo-Classicism
Neo-Classicism is often held to be the opposite of Romanticism. The Neo-Classical period occurs just before the Romantic one, after the Restoration (the return of King Charles II from exile) in 1660. The literature of this period was characterized by a desire to closely imitate the forms of the classical periods of ancient Greece and Rome, such as the epic, tragedy, satire, pastoral and comic. These forms were strictly adhered to and innovation and originality were less prized than imitation; art's purpose was to hold a mirror up to life and emphasis was placed on man as a social being and on his limits.

Ode

A particularly popular poetic form in the period, the most famous examples of which are Keats's odes of 1819. The ode was a classical form, which had developed into the irregular form during the seventeenth century; this was the form used by Wordsworth in 'Ode: Intimations of Immortality'. In contrast, Keats's 'To Autumn' is a Horatian ode, modelled on the odes of the Roman poet Horace. Odes tend to be serious in their subject matter and elevated in style; Keats's odes often present a solitary moment of introspection sparked off by an external source, whether natural (the song of the nightingale) or man-made (a Grecian urn).

Orientalism

The study of the culture and arts of the Middle East, Far East and South Asia undertaken by such prominent figures as William Jones, an orientalist scholar. This work influenced the 'orientalist' writings of Byron, Coleridge, Thomas Moore, Percy Shelley and Robert Southey. *Orientalism* is also the title of Edward Said's 1978 book, in which he showed that the study of countries under imperial rule had produced false and romanticized misrepresentations of the East for ideological purposes.

Pantheism

The belief in an immanent God who exists within the physical world. Wordsworth's early pantheistic tendencies can be seen in lines such as these from 'Tintern Abbey', when the poet feels, as he looks upon nature, 'A presence that disturbs me [. . .] a sense sublime / Of something far more deeply interfused' (*Norton* 2006, Vol. 2: 260).

Periodicals

Periodicals were review magazines which came out at regular intervals, usually quarterly. During the Romantic period, this form came into its own, and the reviews themselves developed from the mere notices they had been previously into opinionated and closely argued engagements with the texts under review. As the number of books being published and literacy rose, these were relied upon far more to direct the reader. The journals aligned themselves with political tendencies and were instrumental in conveying nationalistic, patriotic and dissenting voices.

Picturesque
A new way of thinking about landscape, considering it for the qualities it possessed that might suit a painting. The *Oxford English Dictionary* defines the term as 'having the elements or qualities of a picture; suitable for a picture'. Picturesque gardening was the arranging of a garden so as to resemble a picture, aiming for an irregular or rugged beauty, a kind of artificial naturalness. (See also **the sublime and the beautiful**.)

Sensibility
The capacity for deep feeling for others and the natural world, often associated particularly with women, though it had previously been associated with men, as in Henry Mackenzie's novel *The Man of Feeling* (1771). Excessive sensibility is criticized in Mary Wollstonecraft's *Vindication of the Rights of Woman* as a disease of the rich woman who has nothing to occupy her mind.

Sublime and the beautiful
The aesthetic terms used by Edmund Burke in his 1757 *Enquiry into the Sublime and Beautiful*. The sublime in Burke's formulation is awe-inspiring and transports the viewer, recognizing in the experience a power beyond themselves. The beautiful, however, is soft and small, something which pleases but which the viewer feels he/she has control of rather than being controlled by it, as is the case in an encounter with the sublime. These definitions are gendered, with the sublime imagined as masculine power and the beautiful as feminine.

FURTHER READING AND RESOURCES

General Romanticism

Jarvis, R. (2004) *The Romantic Period: The Intellectual and Cultural Context of English Literature, 1789–1830*. Harlow: Longman.
This is an excellent introduction to the context of Romanticism, using original primary materials to reconsider the period.

McCalman, I. (2001) *An Oxford Companion to the Romantic Age*. Oxford: Oxford University Press.
A compendium of information about the Romantic period, compiled by historians and literary scholars. Considers Romantic-period culture in its broadest possible sense.

Roe, N. (ed.) (2005) *Romanticism: An Oxford Guide*. Oxford: Oxford University Press.
Forty-seven specially commissioned chapters written by experts in particular fields. This book covers a great many subjects in detail and offers a list of further reading at the end of each section.

Romanticism
Journal of Romantic culture and criticism, published by Edinburgh University Press, founded in 1995.

Stabler, J. (2002) *From Burke to Byron, Barbauld to Baillie, 1790–1830*. Basingstoke: Palgrave.
An excellent introduction to the period's literature, which reads the texts carefully while also placing them into historical and other contexts. Stabler uses less canonical figures such as Anna Barbauld, John Clare and William Cobbett alongside Byron and Austen.

Historical, cultural and intellectual context

Politics and economics

Bainbridge, S. (2003) *British Poetry and the Revolutionary and Napoleonic Wars: Visions of Conflict*. Oxford: Oxford University Press.
Argues that the Revolutionary and Napoleonic wars had a significant impact on poetic practices and theories in the Romantic period, and examines a wide range of writers canonical

(Wordsworth, Coleridge and Byron) and non-canonical (Smith, Southey, Scott and Hemans).

Baycroft, T. (1998) *Nationalism in Europe, 1789–1945.* Cambridge: Cambridge University Press.

A user-friendly account of the rise of nationalism and national identities, beginning with the French Revolution.

Dawson, G. (1994) *Soldier Heroes: British Adventure, Empire and the Imagining of Masculinities.* London and New York: Routledge.

A very good account of Scott's *Waverley* in the context of fantasies about empire building, masculinity and nationalism.

Doyle, W. (2001) *The French Revolution: A Very Short Introduction.* Oxford: Oxford University Press.

A short and very readable account, which gives a good sense of the major events and developments of the revolution.

Fulford, T. and Kitson, P. (eds) (1996) *Romanticism and Colonialism: Writing and Empire, 1780–1830.* Cambridge: Cambridge University Press.

This collection of essays investigates topics from slavery to tropical disease, religion and commodity production, and covers a wide range of writers from Edmund Burke to Hannah More, William Blake to Phyllis Wheatley, Olaudah Equiano to Mary Shelley, and Thomas Clarkson to Lord Byron.

Thompson, E. P. (1963) *The Making of the English Working Class.* London: V. Gollancz.

First published in 1963 but republished many times since, this remains one of the best accounts of the political and social conditions of the Romantic period.

Shaw, P. (2002) *Waterloo and the Romantic Imagination.* Basingstoke: Palgrave Macmillan.

Looks at the impact of the Battle of Waterloo on Romantic ideas of individual and national identity and the representation of the dead and wounded in poetry, painting and prose of the period.

Philosophy and religion

Dent, N. (2005) *Rousseau.* London and New York: Routledge.

A readable introduction to Rousseau's life and major works.

Piper, H. W. (1962) *The Active Universe: Pantheism and the Concept of Imagination in the English Romantic Poets.* London: The Athlone Press.

Reveals the importance of pantheism to the early Romantics.

Priestman, M. (1999) *Romantic Atheism: Poetry and Freethought, 1730–1830*. Cambridge: Cambridge University Press.

An excellent account of atheism in the period, dealing with Blake, Coleridge, Erasmus Darwin, Richard Payne Knight and Percy Shelley among others.

Porter, R. (2001) *The Enlightenment*. Basingstoke: Palgrave.

A short and accessible account of the Enlightenment.

Science and technology

Bewell, A. (1999) *Romanticism and Colonial Disease*. Baltimore and London: Johns Hopkins University Press.

Considers the impact of colonialism in terms of epidemic disease, adding much to our knowledge and understanding of the historical and colonial context of the period's literature.

Golinski, J. (1992) *Science as Public Culture*. Cambridge: Cambridge University Press.

Tracks the emergence of scientific disciplines from the egalitarian and philanthropic aims of Priestley to the centers of institutional science.

Knight, D. (1992) *Humphry Davy: Science and Power*. Oxford: Blackwell.

A lively account of one of the most interesting of Romantic scientists, charting his rise from provincial science circles to the Royal Institution in London.

Uglow, J. (2002) *The Lunar Men: The Friends Who Made the Future*. London: Faber and Faber.

An excellent account of the scientists, doctors and industrialists who made up the Midlands' Lunar Society, including Erasmus Darwin, Matthew Boulton, James Watt, Josiah Wedgwood, Thomas Day and Richarch Lovell Edgeworth.

Arts and culture

Barrell, J. (1980) *The Dark Side of Landscape of the Landscape: The Rural Poor in English Painting 1730–1840*. Cambridge: Cambridge University Press.

Although it was published some time ago, this book remains influential.

Blaney Brown, D. (2001) *Romanticism*. New York: Phaidon.

A beautiful book, with many colour pictures, and a wide-ranging discussion of the art produced in this period.

Fulford, T., Lee, D. and Kitson, P. (2004) *Literature, Science and Exploration in the Romantic Era*. Cambridge: Cambridge University Press.

Reveals the scientific and colonial interests of explorers in the Romantic period, paying particular attention to Joseph Banks, the President of the Royal Society.

Fulford, T. and Kitson, P. (eds) (2001) *Travels, Explorations and Empires: Writings from the Era of Imperial Expansion, 1770–1835*. 8 vols. London: Pickering and Chatto.

A collection of travel narratives from the Romantic period.

Leask, N. (1992) *British Romantic Writers and the East: Anxieties of Empire*. Cambridge: Cambridge University Press.

A highly influential account of 'orientalist' representations of the 'East' in the work of Byron, Coleridge, de Quincey and Percy Shelley.

Romantic literature

Major genres

Burroughs, C. (ed.) (2000) *Women in British Romantic Theatre: Drama, Performance, and Society, 1790–1840*. Cambridge: Cambridge University Press.

This is the first collection of essays to examine the extraordinary contribution of women playwrights, actors, translators, critics and managers who worked in British theatre during the romantic period, focusing on women well known during their day but who have been neglected for some 150 years.

Clery, E. (1995) *The Rise of Supernatural Fiction, 1762–1800*. Cambridge: Cambridge University Press.

Questioning what the historical reasons are for supernatural fiction's growing popularity in the late eighteenth century and looking at the Gothic novels of Horace Walpole, Ann Radcliffe, M. G. Lewis and others, this book draws out the connection between fictions of the supernatural and the growth of consumerism.

Clery, E. and Miles, R. (eds) (2000) *Gothic Documents: A Sourcebook, 1700–1820*. Manchester: Manchester University Press.
A collection of source materials and secondary matter on the Gothic.

Cox, J. and Gamer, M. (eds) (2003) *The Broadview Anthology of Romantic Drama*. Ontario: Broadview.
An important anthology of Romantic drama with an excellent introduction to the genre.

Curran, S. (1990) *Poetic Form and British Romanticism*. Oxford: Oxford University Press.
Considers the Romantics' appropriation of certain genres, whether the revival of lost forms, a preoccupation with fixed forms, such as the ode, or their reconception of major genres like the pastoral, the epic and the romance.

Everest, K. (1990) *English Romantic Poetry: An Introduction to the Literary Scene*. Milton Keynes: Open University Press.
Very usefully sets out the literary scene in which the Romantic poets published, though only really deals with the male poets.

Furniss, T. and Bath, M. (1996) *Reading Poetry: An Introduction*. Harlow: Longman.
Although this is an introduction to poetry in general, it has useful sections on genre (including the ballad) and context.

O'Flynn, P. (2000) *How to Study Romantic Poetry*. Basingstoke: Palgrave Macmillan.
Considers the genre of poetry and is a very hands-on kind of book, offering practical advice on how to read and write on Romantic poetry.

Punter, D. (2000) *The Blackwell Companion to the Gothic*. Oxford: Blackwell.
Twenty-five essays organized into five sections: Gothic Backgrounds; the 'Original' Gothic; Nineteenth- and Twentieth-century Transmutations; Ideas about the Gothic; and the Continuing Debate. There is also an extensive bibliography of primary and secondary materials.

Wolfson, S. (1997) *Formal Charges: The Shaping of Poetry in British Romanticism*. Stanford, CA: Stanford University Press.
A highly successful attempt to reconcile formalist and historicist readings of Romantic poetry.

Movements and literary groups

Cox, J. N. (1998) *Poetry and Politics in the Cockney School: Keats, Shelley, Hunt, and Their Circle*. Cambridge: Cambridge University Press.

An important account of the centrality of Leigh Hunt in the formation of the poetry of the 'Cockney School'.

Klancher, J. (1987) *The Making of English Reading Audiences, 1790–1832*. Madison, WI: University of Wisconsin Press.

An excellent account of the way that reviewing in the period influences the literature produced.

Parker, M. (2000) *Literary Magazines and British Romanticism*. Cambridge: Cambridge University Press.

Looks at the writing in magazines such as the *London Magazine* and *Blackwood's Edinburgh Magazine* to see how a dynamic culture developed.

Russell, G. and Tuite, C. (eds) (2002) *Romantic Sociability: Social Networks and Literary Culture in Britain, 1770–1840*. Cambridge: Cambridge University Press.

A collection of essays influenced by Habermas's notion of the emergence of the 'public sphere' in the eighteenth century. The essays reveal the sociability of the Romantic writers, their networks and coteries.

Critical approaches

Historical overview

Abrams, M. H. (1975) *English Romantic Poets: Modern Essays in Criticism*. 2nd edn. Oxford: Oxford University Press.

Selections from some of the most influential critical perspectives on Romanticism written throughout the twentieth century.

Gleckner, R. F. and Enscoe, G. E. (eds) (1970) *Romanticism: Points of View*. 2nd edn. New Jersey: Prentice-Hall.

A collection of essays ranging from Walter Pater to Earl R. Wasserman.

Current issues and debates

Chandler, J. (1996) *England in 1819: The Politics of Literary Culture and the Case of Romantic Historicism*. Chicago: University of Chicago Press.

Argues that the Romantics themselves were peculiarly aware of historicism.

Coleman, D. (2005) *Romantic Colonization and British Anti-Slavery.* Cambridge: Cambridge University Press.

Considers the effect of the loss of the British transatlantic empire on the discussions of colonialism and the anti-slavery movement.

Levinson, M., Butler, M., McGann, M. and Hamilton, P. (1989) *Rethinking Historicism: Critical Readings in Romantic History.* Oxford: Blackwell.

Essays written by four of the main proponents of the new historicist method in Romanticism.

Makdisi, S. (1998) *Romantic Imperialism: Universal Empire and the Culture of Modernity.* Cambridge: Cambridge University Press.

Traces the emergence of new forms of imperialism and capitalism in the period, via readings of Wordsworth, Blake, Byron, Shelley and Scott.

Roe, N. (ed.) (1995) *Keats and History.* Cambridge: Cambridge University Press.

An important work that refuses to see Keats as an escapist poet and instead reveals that his poetry was engaged with the political and historical circumstances of its composition.

Electronic resources

General romanticism
The Corvey Project
www.shu.ac.uk/schools/cs/corvey/

Hosted by Sheffield Hallam University, which has microfiche collection of rare and unique works from the Corvey library in Germany. The website contains a searchable database, 'Corvey Women Writers on the Web: an Electronic Guide to Literature, 1796–1834' and also the journal *CW3*.

Eighteenth-Century Collections Online
www.gale.com/EighteenthCentury/

A digitization project that your library may have subscribed to, which claims to have digitized 'every significant English-language and foreign-language title printed in Great Britain during the eighteenth century'. While there definitely are omissions this is an incredible resource, making many rare books, pamphlets, plays and collections of poems available online.

Literature Compass

www.literature-compass.com

If your library subscribes to this, you will be able to read the articles published in the Romanticism journal, edited by Elizabeth Fay and Sharon Ruston. If not, you are able to pay to view single articles.

Literature Encyclopaedia

www.litencyc.com/index.php

Articles written on primary texts, critical accounts and authors. The Romantic period is well served with some good, short introductions to works.

Romantic Circles

www.rc.umd.edu/

This is a major resource, edited by Neil Fraistat and Steven E. Jones, which is constantly being added to. It hosts digital editions of several texts, a blog, chronologies, concordances and much more.

Romantic Chronology

english.ucsb.edu:591/rchrono/

A densely detailed chronology of the period.

Romanticism on the Net

www.ron.umontreal.ca/

The first online Romanticism journal, published since 1996. The site includes articles published in the journal plus a good list of links and book reviews.

Historical, cultural and intellectual context

Politics and Economics

A Digital Resource for the Act of Union (1800)

www.actofunion.ac.uk/

A virtual library with a searchable collection of pamphlets, newspapers, parliamentary papers and manuscript material contemporary with the 1800 Act of Union between Ireland and Britain.

Brycchan Carey on Slavery, Abolition and Emancipation

www.brycchancarey.com/slavery/index.htm

The website of Brycchan Carey (2005), author of *British Abolitionism and the Rhetoric of Sensibility: Writing, Sentiment, and Slavery, 1760–1807*. Basingstoke: Palgrave Macmillan. Contains a list of resources in this area, plus biographies, poems about slavery, information about abolitionists and resources specific to Ignatius Sancho, Olaudah Equiano and Quobna Ottobah Cugoano.

Merseyside Maritime Museum, Transatlantic Slavery: Against Human Dignity

www.liverpoolmuseums.org.uk/maritime/slavery/

The website for a gallery dedicated to presenting the history of the slave trade.

The Age of George III

www.historyhome.co.uk/

Gives information on the period of King George III's reign (1760–1820), including the ministries that ran the country, events in Ireland and America, India, France and Britain.

Arts and culture

The William Blake Archive

www.blakearchive.org/blake/

James Gillray: The Art of Caricature

www.tate.org.uk/britain/exhibitions/gillray/default.htm

This is the website for a Gillray exhibition at the Tate Britain Gallery held in London in 2001. It collects together many of Gillray's cartoons under themes and by character.

Turner Online at the Tate Britain Gallery, London

www.tate.org.uk/britain/turner/default.htm

Features a brief biography of the artist, and a timeline which locates some of the most important dates in the artist's life alongside other significant political and cultural events. There are also discussions of Turner by artists, critics, historians and others.

Romantic literature

Major genres

Koelzer, R. (2006) The Poetics of 'Divine Chit-Chat': Rethinking the Conversation Poems', *Literature Compass*. Available from www.literature-compass.com.
> This is a specific survey of the conversation poem, offering a good bibliography as well as a reading of an example of the genre.

Movements and literary groups

The Bluestocking Archive
www.faculty.umb.edu/elizabeth_fay/archive2.html
> Maintained by Elizabeth Fay, this website contains works by and about the Bluestockings.

The John Clare Page
www.johnclare.info/default.html
> A selection of Clare's poems and prose, as well as offering a chronology, portraits of Clare, essays written about him and a survey of criticism.

Dictionary of Sensibility
www.engl.virginia.edu/enec981/dictionary/intro.html
> The list of terms associated with sensibility on this website is particularly useful.

Goodridge, J. (ed.) (2006) *A Biographical & Bibliographical Database of British and Irish Labouring-Class Poets 1700–1900* is available at: http://human.ntu.ac.uk/research/labouringclasswriters/elsie1.htm

Labouring-Class Writers
http://human.ntu.ac.uk/research/labouringclasswriters/default.htm
> This website contains links to the Thomas Chatterton and Robert Bloomfield webpages as well as an extensive database of labouring-class writers from the period.

Periodicals Archive Online
http://pao.chadwyck.co.uk/home.do
> This website has the *Edinburgh Review* online so that you can view controversial reviews and search the *Edinburgh Review* for yourself.

The *Quarterly Review* Archive
www.rc.umd.edu/reference/qr/index.html
    See the reviews published by the *Quarterly* for yourself; volumes
    1 (1809) to 31 (1824) are published here, with a searchable index
    and transcriptions of John Murray's and William Gifford's cor-
    respondence.

Works cited

Primary

Aiken, J. and Barbauld, A. (1773) On the Pleasure Derived
    from Objects of Terror, with Sir Bertrand, a Fragment. In
    Miscellaneous Pieces [online]. London: J. Johnson. Available from:
    <www.english.upenn.edu/~mgamer/Etexts/barbauldessays.h
    tml> [accessed 9 April 2006].

Anon. (1776) 'Observations on female literature in general,
    including some particulars relating to Mrs. Montagu and Mrs.
    Barbauld'. *The Westminster Magazine*, pp. 283–5. Available from:
    www.rc.umd.edu/editions/contemps/barbauld/poems1773/
    criticism/duncombe.html> [Accessed 18 April 2006].

Anon. (1799) *The British Critic*, 14, pp. 623–7.

Anon. (1809) 'Letter from "Amicus" to Mr Urban on Thomas
    Beddoes's death'. *The Gentleman's Magazine*, 79, p. 120.

Anon. (1814) 'An Inquiry into the Probability and Rationality of
    Mr. Hunter's Theory of Life; being the subject of the first Two
    Anatomical Lectures delivered before the Royal College of
    Surgeons, of London. By John Abernethy'. *Edinburgh Review*, 23,
    pp. 384–98.

Anon. (1834) 'On the Connexion of the Physical Sciences. By Mrs.
    Somerville'. *Quarterly Review*, 51, pp. 54–68.

Barbauld, A. (1773) *Poems*. London: J. Johnson. L. Vargo and
    A. Muri (eds). Available from: <www.rc.umd.edu/editions/-
    contemps/barbauld/poems1773> [Accessed 18 April 2006].

Browning, R. (1981) *The Complete Works of Robert Browning*. R. A.
    King, J. Herring, P. Honan, A.N. Kincaid and A.C. Dooley
    (eds), 16 vols. Athens, OH: Ohio University Press.

Burke, E. (1999) *The Portable Edmund Burke*. Isaac Kramnick (ed.).
    Harmondsworth: Penguin.

Burns, R. (1786) *Poems, Chiefly in the Scottish Dialect*. Kilmarnock: John Wilson.

Byron, G. (1986) *The Complete Poetical Works*. J. J. McGann (ed.), 7 vols. Oxford: Clarendon Press.

Dalton, J. (1808) *New System of Chemical Philosophy*. 2 vols. London: R. Bickerstaff.

Darwin, E. (1791) *The Botanic Garden*. London: J. Johnson.

Davy, H. (1799) 'Experimental essays on heat, light, and on the combinations of light, with a new theory of respiration, and observations on the chemistry of life'. In Thomas Beddoes and James Watt (eds). *Contributions to Physical and Medical Knowledge, Principally from the West of England*. London: Longman and Rees, pp. 5–147.

Davy, H. (1800) *Researches, Chemical and Philosophical, Chiefly Concerning Nitrous Oxide, or Dephlogisticated Nitrous Air, and its Respiration*. London: J. Johnson.

Galvani, L. (1953) *De Veribus Elicitatis in Moto Musculari Commentarius*. Trans. by R. Montraville Green. Cambridge, MA: Elizabeth Licht.

Godwin, W. (1982) *Caleb Williams*. 2nd edn. David McCracken (ed.). Oxford: Oxford University Press.

Hazlitt, W. (1991) *The Spirit of the Age*. E. D. Mackerness (ed.). Plymouth: Northcote House.

Jeffrey, F. (1803) 'Southey's Thalaba; A Metrical Romance'. *Edinburgh Review*, 1:1, pp. 63–83.

Jeffrey, F. (1807) 'Poems, in Two Volumes. By W. Wordsworth'. *Edinburgh Review*, 11:21, pp. 214–31.

Keats, J. (1959) *Selected Letters and Poems*. D. Bush (ed.). Boston: Houghton Mifflin.

Lawrence, W. (1819) *Lectures on Physiology, Zoology, and The Natural History of Man, delivered at the Royal College of Surgeons*. London: J. Callow.

de la Mettrie, J. (1996) *Machine Man and Other Writings*. Trans. Ann Thompson (ed.). Cambridge: Cambridge University Press.

More, H. (1782) *Sensibility. A Poetical Epistle to the Hon. Mrs Boscawen*. Available from: <www.english.upenn.edu/~mgamer/Etexts/more.html> [Accessed 15 April 2006].

More, H. (1787) *The Bas Bleu.* Available from: <www.english.upenn. edu/~curran/250-96/Sensibility/morebas.html> [Accessed 15 April 2006].

Paine, T. (1995) *Common Sense. In Rights of Man, Common Sense and Other Political Writings,* Mark Philp (ed.). Oxford: Oxford University Press.

Paley, W. (1802) *Natural Theology.* London: Faulder.

Peacock, T. L. (2001) 'The Four Ages of Poetry'. In *The Norton Anthology of Theory and Criticism.* V. B. Leitch (ed.), pp. 684–94. New York and London: W. W. Norton.

Price, U. (1974) *An Essay on the Picturesque* [online]. London: J. Robson. Available from <http://galenet.galegroup.com/servlet/ECCO> [Accessed 10 April 2006].

Robinson, M. (2000) *Selected Poems,* Judith Pascoe (ed.). Ontario: Broadview.

Shelley, M. (1987) *The Journals of Mary Shelley.* P. R. Feldman and D. Scott-Kilvert (eds). Baltimore and London: The Johns Hopkins University Press.

Shelley, M. (1994) *Frankenstein.* D. L. Macdonald and Kathleen Scherf (eds). Ontario: Broadview Press.

Shelley, P. B. (1964) *The Letters of Percy Bysshe Shelley.* F. L. Jones (ed.). 2 vols. Oxford: Clarendon Press.

Shelley, P. B. (1970) *Poetical Works.* Thomas Hutchinson (ed.), G. M. Matthews (corr.). Oxford: Oxford University Press.

Shelley, P. B. (1977) *Shelley's Poetry and Prose.* D. H. Reiman and S. Powers (eds). New York and London: W. W. Norton.

Southey, R. (1965) *New Letters of Robert Southey.* K. Curry (ed.). 2 vols. New York and London: Columbia University Press.

Walpole, H. (1986) *The Castle of Otranto.* In *Three Gothic Novels,* P. Fairclough (ed.). Harmondsworth: Penguin.

Wollstonecraft, M. (1989) *The Works of Mary Wollstonecraft.* J. Todd and M. Butler (eds). 7 vols. London: William Pickering.

Wollstonecraft, M. (1997) *A Vindication of the Rights of Woman.* In *The Vindications,* D. L. MacDonald and K. Scherf (eds). Ontario: Broadview.

Secondary

Abrams, M. H. (1953) *The Mirror and the Lamp*. Oxford: Oxford University Press.

Abrams, M. H. (ed.) (2000) *The Norton Anthology of English Literature.* 2 vols, 7th edn. New York and London: W. W. Norton.

Anderson, B. (1991) *Imagined Communities: Reflections on the Origin and Spread of Nationalism* London: Verso.

Armstrong, I. (2001) 'Natural and National Monuments – Felicia Heman's "The Image in Lava": A Note'. In *Felicia Hemans: Reimagining Poetry in the Nineteenth Century*, N. Sweet and J. Melynk (eds), pp. 212–30. Basingstoke: Palgrave.

Arasse, D. (1989) *The Guillotine and the Terror*, Christopher Miller (trans.). Harmondsworth: Penguin.

Arnold, M. (1964) *Essays in Criticism*. London: J. M. Dent.

Barker-Benfield, G. J. (2001) 'Sensibility'. In *An Oxford Companion to the Romantic Age*, I. McCalman (ed.), pp. 102–14. Oxford: Oxford University Press.

Barthes, R. (2001) 'The Death of the Author'. In *The Norton Anthology of Theory and Criticism* V. B. Leitch (ed.), pp. 1466–70. New York and London: W. W. Norton.

Baycroft, T. (1998) *Nationalism in Europe, 1789–1945*. Cambridge: Cambridge University Press.

Bieri, J. (2005) *Percy Bysshe Shelley: A Biography*. New Jersey: Associated University Presses.

Bloom, H. (2001) 'The Anxiety of Influence'. In *The Norton Anthology of Theory and Criticism*. V. B. Leitch (ed.), pp. 1797–1805. New York and London: W. W. Norton.

Bode, C. (2005) 'Europe'. In *Romanticism: An Oxford Guide*, N. Roe (ed.), pp. 126–36. Oxford: Oxford University Press.

Butler, M. (1981) *Romantics, Rebels and Reactionaries: English Literature and its Background, 1760–1830*. Oxford: Oxford University Press.

Chandler, J. (1988) *England in 1819*. Chicago: University of Chicago Press.

Coleman, D. (2002) 'Firebrands, Letters and Flowers: Mrs Barbauld and the Priestleys'. In *Romantic Sociability*, G. Russell and C. Tuite (eds), pp. 82–103. Cambridge: Cambridge University Press.

Coleman, D. (2005) 'Post-colonialism'. In *Romanticism: An Oxford Guide*, N. Roe (ed.), pp. 237–48. Oxford: Oxford University Press.

Cox, J. and Gamer, M. (eds) (2003) *The Broadview Anthology of Romantic Drama*. Ontario: Broadview.

Cox, J. (1999) 'Leigh Hunt's Cockney School: The Lakers' "Other" '. *Romanticism on the Net*, 14. Available at: <www.erudit.org/revue/ron/1999/v/n14/005859ar.html> [Accessed 18 April 2006].

Crouch, L. E. (1978) 'Davy's *A Discourse Introductory to a Course of Lectures on Chemistry*: A Possible Scientific Source of *Frankenstein*'. *Keats-Shelley Journal*, 27, pp. 35–44.

Curran, S. (1996) 'Romantic Poetry: The I Altered'. In *Romantic Writings*, Stephen Bygrave (ed.), pp. 279–93. London: Routledge.

Douglas-Fairhurst, R. (2002) *Victorian Afterlives The Shaping of Influence in Nineteenth-Century Literature*. Oxford: Oxford University Press.

Eliot, T. S. (1964) 'Shelley and Keats'. In *The Use of Poetry and the Use of Criticism*, pp. 87–102. London: Faber.

Eliot, T. S. (2001) 'Tradition and the Individual Talent'. In *The Norton Anthology of Theory and Criticism*, V. B. Leitch (ed.), pp. 1092–8. New York and London: W. W. Norton.

Fay, E. (1998) *A Feminist Introduction to Romanticism*. Oxford: Blackwell.

Feldman, P. R. and T. M. Kelley (eds) (1995) *Romantic Women Writers: Voices and Countervoices*. Hanover, NH: University Press of New England.

Fulford, T. (2001) 'Wordworth's "The Haunted Tree" and the Sexual Politics of Landscape'. In *Placing and Displacing Romanticism*, P. Kitson (ed.), pp. 33–47. Hampshire: Ashgate.

Fulford, T., Lee, D. and Kitson, P. (2004) *Literature, Science and Exploration in the Romantic Era*. Cambridge: Cambridge University Press.

Gay, P. (2002) *Jane Austen and the Theatre*. Cambridge: Cambridge University Press.

Golinski, J. (1992) *Science as Public Culture*. Cambridge: Cambridge University Press.

Goodridge, J (ed.) (2006) 'A Biographical & Bibliographical Database of British and Irish Labouring-Class Poets 1700–1900'. Version 6.2. Available at: <http://human.ntu.ac. uk/research/labouringclasswriters/elsie1.htm> [Accessed 9 April 2006].

Goodridge, J. and Keegan, B. (2004) 'John Clare and labouring-class verse'. In *The Cambridge Companion to English Literature, 1740–1830*, T. Keymer and J. Mee (eds), pp. 280–96. Cambridge: Cambridge University Press.

Greenblatt, S. (gen. ed.) (2006) *The Norton Anthology of English Literature*, 2 vols, 8th edn. New York and London: W. W. Norton.

Grenby, M. O. (2001) *The Anti-Jacobin Novel: British Conservatism and the French Revolution*. Cambridge: Cambridge University Press.

Habermas, J. (1962) *The Structural Transformation of the Public Sphere*. Reprint edition, 1991. Cambridge, MA: MIT Press.

Hartman, G. (1993) 'Romanticism and Anti-Self-Consciousness'. In *Romanticism*, C. Chase (ed.), pp. 43–54. London and New York: Longman.

Haslett, M. (2003) *Pope to Burney, 1714–1779: Scriblerians to Bluestockings*. Hampshire: Palgrave Macmillan.

Hulme, T. E. (1970) 'Romanticism and Classicism'. In *Romanticism: Points of View*, R. F. Gleckner and G. E. Enscoe (ed), pp. 55–65. 2nd edn. New Jersey: Prentice-Hall, 1970.

Hutton, J. (1795) *Theory of the Earth with Proofs and Illustrations*. 2 vols. Edinburgh: William Creech.

Janowitz, A. (2002) 'Amiable and radical sociability: Anna Barbauld's "free familiar conversation" '. In *Romantic Sociability*, G. Russell and C. Tuite (eds), pp. 62–82. Cambridge: Cambridge University Press.

Janowitz, A. (2004) *Women Romantic Poets: Anna Barbauld and Mary Robinson*. Devon: Northcote House.

Jarvis, R. (2004) *The Romantic Period: The Intellectual and Cultural Context of English Literature, 1789–1830*. Harlow: Pearson.

Johnston, K. R. (2005) 'New Historicism'. In *Romanticism: An Oxford Guide*. N. Roe (ed.), pp. 165–81. Oxford: Oxford University Press.

Jones, V. (1990) *Women in the Eighteenth Century: Constructions of Femininity*. London: Routledge.

Kelly, G. (2000) 'Politicising the Personal: Mary Wollstonecraft,

Mary Shelley'. In *Mary Shelley In Her Times*, B. T. Bennett and S. Curran (eds), pp. 147–59. Baltimore: Johns Hopkins University Press.

Knight, D. (1992) *Humphry Davy: Science and Power*. Oxford: Blackwell.

Kucich, G. (2004) 'Keats, Shelley, Byron, and the Hunt Circle'. In *The Cambridge Companion to English Literature, 1740–1830*, T. Keymer and J. Mee (eds), pp. 263–79. Cambridge: Cambridge University Press.

Labbe, J. (2000) 'The Anthologised Romance of Della Crusca and Anna Matilda'. *Romanticism on the Net*, 18. Available at: <http://users.ox.ac.uk/~scat0385/18labbe. html> [Accessed 11 April 2006].

Larrisy, E. (1985) *William Blake*. Oxford: Blackwell.

Leavis, F. R. (1936) *Revaluation: Tradition and Development in English Poetry*. London: Chatto and Windus.

Leitch, V. B. (ed.) (2001) *The Norton Anthology of Theory and Criticism*. New York and London: W. W. Norton.

Lewis, C. S. (1975) 'Shelley, Dryden and Mr Eliot'. In *English Romantic Poets: Modern Essays in Criticism*, M. H. Abrams (ed.), pp. 324–44. 2nd edn. Oxford: Oxford University Press.

Lovejoy, A. O. (1970) 'On the Discrimination of Romanticisms'. In *Romanticism: Points of View*, R. F. Gleckner and G. E. Enscoe (eds), pp. 66–81. 2nd edn. New Jersey: Prentice-Hall.

McCalman, I. (ed.) (2001) *An Oxford Companion to the Romantic Age*. Oxford: Oxford University Press.

Mellor, A. (1988) *Mary Shelley: Her Life, her Fiction, her Monsters*. New York and London: Routledge.

Mellor, A. (1993) *Romanticism and Gender*. New York and London: Routledge.

McGann, J. (1983) *The Romantic Ideology: A Critical Investigation*. Chicago: University of Chicago Press.

McKusick, J. (2005) 'Ecology'. In *Romanticism: An Oxford Guide*, N. Roe (ed.), pp. 199–218. Oxford: Oxford University Press.

Moers, E. (1976) *Literary Women*. New York: Doubleday.

Motion, A. (1997) *Keats*. London: Faber and Faber.

Norris, C. (2002) *Deconstruction*. 3rd edn. New York and London: Routledge.

Roe, N. (ed.) (2005) *Romanticism: An Oxford Guide*. Oxford: Oxford University Press.

Roe, N. (1997) *Keats and the Culture of Dissent*. Oxford: Oxford University Press.

Ross, M. (1994) 'Configurations of Feminine Reform: The Woman Writer and the Tradition of Dissent'. In *Re-Visioning Romanticism: British Women Writers 1776–1837*, C. Shiner Wilson and J. Haeffner (eds). Philadelphia: University of Pennsylvania Press.

Russell, G. and Tuite, C. (eds) (2002) *Romantic Sociability: Social Networks and Literary Culture in Britain, 1770–1840*. Cambridge: Cambridge University Press.

Ruston, S. (2005) *Shelley and Vitality*. Basingstoke: Palgrave Macmillan.

Said, E. (1978) *Orientalism*. New York: Pantheon.

Scrivener, M. (2001) 'Jacobian Romanticism: John Thelwall's "Wye" Essay and "Pedestrian Excursion" (1779–1801)'. In *Placing and Displacing Romanticism*, P. Kitson (ed.), pp. 73–87. Hampshire: Ashgate.

Selden, R., P. Widdowson and P. Brooker (1997) *A Reader's Guide to Contemporary Literary Criticism*. 4th edn. London: Prentice Hall.

Stafford, F. (2005) 'England, Ireland, Scotland, Wales'. In *Romanticism: An Oxford Guide*, N. Roe (ed.), pp. 114–25. Oxford: Oxford University Press.

Steyaert, K. (1999) 'Mediumistic Shelley Sonnets in the Netherlands'. In *The Influence and Anxiety of the British Romantics: Spectres of Romanticism*, Sharon Ruston (ed.), pp. 199–224. Lewiston: Edwin Mellen.

Stillinger, J. (2001) 'The Story of Keats'. In *The Cambridge Companion to Keats*, S. Wolfson (ed.), pp. 246–61. Cambridge: Cambridge University Press.

Wells, R. (2001) 'Famine'. In *An Oxford Companion to the Romantic Age*, I. McCalman (ed.), pp. 504–5. Oxford: Oxford University Press.

Williams, C. (2001) ' "Inhumanly Brought Back to Life and Misery": Mary Wollstonecraft, *Frankenstein*, and the Royal Humane Society'. *Women's Writing*, 8:2, pp. 213–34.

Williams, J. (2000) *Mary Shelley: A Literary Life*. Basingstoke: Macmillan.

Wootton, S. (1999) 'Ghastly Visualities: Keats and Victorian Art'. In *The Influence and Anxiety of the British Romantics: Spectres of Romanticism*, Sharon Ruston (ed.), pp. 159–80. Lewiston: Edwin Mellen.

Wu, D. (ed.) (2006) *Romanticism: An Anthology*. 3rd edn. Oxford: Blackwell.

Zimmerman, S. (2004) 'Smith Charlotte (1749–1806)'. In *The Oxford Dictionary of National Biography* [online]. 2nd edn. Oxford: Oxford University Press. Available from: <http://0-www.oxforddnb.com.unicat.bangor.ac.uk:80/view/article/257 90> [Accessed 30 Jan 2006].

Index